D1081774

The Tree of World Religions

John Bellaimey

2018

Front Edge Publishing

For more information and further discussion, visit ...

My site:
www.treeofworldreligions.com

Our school:
www.breckschool.org

My blog:
https://treesandrivers.blog

My TED-Ed talk on yin & yang:
https://youtu.be/ezmR9Attpyc

My TED-Ed talk on 5 religions:
https://youtu.be/m6dCxo7t_aE

Front Edge Publishing specializes in speed and flexibility in adapting and updating our books. We can include links to video and other online media. We offer discounts on bulk purchases for special events, corporate training, and small groups. We are able to customize bulk orders by adding corporate or event logos on the cover and we can include additional pages inside describing your event or corporation. For more information about our fast and flexible publishing or permission to use our materials, please contact Front Edge Publishing at info@FrontEdgePublishing.com.

Table of Contents

PART ONE

The Roots of Religion

We can't see the roots of a tree unless we dig, or a windstorm uproots it. The roots spread almost as widely as the branches, and besides anchoring the tree in place, they absorb nutrients and water from the soil. Roots are like the deep structure and nourishment of religion. We start with the human mind, which is where religion lives. With the help of Karen Armstrong, Huston Smith, and John Meagher, you will see that religion is a kind of knowledge, like science or history. Next is a very nerdy chapter on theistic and atheistic reasoning, followed by a chapter where I'll invite you to make your definition of religion a little bigger, so we don't leave some important wisdom out. Then comes Ninian Smart's elegant seven dimensions for comparing religions. Finally, we'll get specific by looking at four indigenous, local religions and at the most basic of all religious stories: Creation.

CHAPTER 1

Older and Newer

I n Karen Armstrong's classic *History of God*, she traces the evolution of the human idea of a higher power from its simplest beginnings to the present, and then points toward the future. Let's assume for now that there really is a God, even though we can't prove it. This not the history of the *actual* H.P. (Higher Power) because none of us were around to record it. This is more correctly called the History of The Idea Of God.

STAGE I: SKY GOD

When our species was young, and our ancestors traveled in bands of hunters and gatherers, we think they believed in a god. It lived in the sky. This god watched human beings, but didn't get involved in our lives. Being nomads, the people built no houses, let alone temples. They probably did not perform sacrifices or even ask for favors in prayer. But punishments, from time to time, came from this Sky God. There are a few remaining simple societies, often isolated in the desert (Kalahari Bushmen) or forest (Mbuti Pygmies) who conceive of God in this way, but for most people today, this Sky God has been replaced.

European "Venus Statues"

STAGE II: GODDESS

When our ancestors discovered agriculture (during the Old Stone Age) they grew to respect and even fear the Earth, asking why we sometimes get the rain we need and sometimes not? Why does this soil produce enough grain and that soil doesn't? They didn't know whether they would succeed, and began to treat fertility as a sacred mystery, a Goddess. This loving Earth-mother gives life to all things, and regulates the cycles of the sun, moon, tides, and seasons. She gets involved, unlike the Sky God, and she cares for humans. The Goddess was usually *personified*, meaning people imagined her as being similar to us. Thousands of small statues of her, pregnant and ready to nurse her children, have been found from Siberia to India to the Middle East, and Europe. Some cultures see her as a feminine energy force, but not a personal Goddess.

STAGE III: POLYTHEISM

Mother Earth and Father Sky didn't vanish, however. The next stage got its start with the building of cities and empires in Ancient Egypt, India, Greece, Central America, and Peru. Mother Earth became known as Ishtar in Babylon, Isis in Egypt, and Aphrodite in Greece. Father Sky was called Zeus in Greece, Itzamna in Mayan, and Odin in Scandinavia.

The Persians may have been the first to describe a perfect world above where everything is done right, as opposed to our own world, filled with suffering. The gods who live there have much to teach us, so humans need to listen and obey. Gods and goddesses appeared who took charge of fire, rain, love, wisdom, and the other forces humans need to deal with. When everyone farmed or herded, each person did many tasks, but when cities developed, people specialized as bakers, tailors, soldiers, or merchants. The gods also branched out, specializing in love, war, wisdom, and so on.

Polytheism has lots of types: if you believe there are lots of gods, but you should just follow YOUR people's god, that's called *monolatry*. But if you believe that there are NO other gods but the One God, that's not polytheism. That's called *monotheism*.

STAGE IV

Beginning with Moses, the monotheistic World Religions developed —Judaism, Christianity, Islam, Daoism, Late Philosophical Hinduism, and Buddhism. Idolatry (worshipping anything else) came to be seen as wrong. In Stage III, idolatry was normal: you worshipped different gods in different situations, or at certain seasons, or in certain temples. Monotheism says: it's all one, even if it looks like many, and acting as if there are various competing gods disrespects the unity of the Divine. One frequent type of monotheism, however, says there is not only one God, but also only one religion: "ours." This is *religious exclusivism*.

STAGE V

The future of the concept of God is uncertain. Many want to declare 'God' dead, but that concept seems to be losing popularity as neuroscience, art, and literature continue to suggest that a "God-shaped-hole" is somehow an innate part of the human mind. Some future mixing of the traditions of east and west seems likelier.

CHAPTER 2

Higher And Lower

Where do we get these ideas about God? Is there a God-gene in our DNA? Prof. Paul Bogard, Breck '84 and author of *The End of Night*, who teaches at James Madison University, thinks spirituality begins with the wonder of a totally dark sky. At night, we look up at the stars and planets, we see the Milky Way, and we feel tiny. The universe is obviously gigantic. The Big Bang was 13-plus billion years ago. All the matter and energy we can measure started then. Whatever there was before the Big Bang is forever invisible behind the noise of the Bang itself. Religious people suspect that God was there, but we do not know how.

Even before we knew how tiny our planet is, our ancestors believed the universe was infinite. Huston Smith says, "if you claim that reality is finite, you come to a door with one side only, and that's absurd." It makes more sense for everything to keep going. Sure, we have to use our imagination, but that's where religion comes in: what does infinity mean? What's reality like, way beyond us? Is it good? Does it care? Can it hurt us?

Most religions describe the universe like the diagram on the next page. Starting in the dark blue center, we find the simplest level of being: plain old Matter (M). Rocks, lightning bolts, water, and other abiotic things. They exist. That's all.

The next circle is light blue: plants. This level has one new power, *life*. They can die. They eat, reproduce, and grow. They don't move (ok, Venus Flytraps move, but not like a frog or a snake).

Then the green circle: animals, who have both of the lower powers (existence and life) plus one new power, *consciousness*, which lets them plan, react, and feel.

And then comes us, in the yellow circle. This level adds one new power, *self-awareness*. We think about our thinking. We have personalities, speak languages, think new thoughts, compose poems about love, and make art. This is the highest

level we can know. Zoologists are learning that some of the higher animals like chimpanzees, dolphins, and magpies may also be at this level, as they can recognize themselves as distinct individuals.

Now the diagram gets into mythology. We don't know what's greater than we are. The orange circle is for angels and demons, ancestors, spirits, Mount Olympus, Narnia — everything between us and the gods. This level includes things that exist, are alive but can't die, have consciousness, self-awareness, and, the new powers we can only imagine. Superpowers. Maybe they can fly or teleport. Perhaps they can watch us, help us, or haunt us. They live in some extra dimensions we cannot see, though our greatest saints have pierced the barrier and seen the glory of higher planes. When we try to describe the level above us, at first we come up with superhumans: gods who can fly or spirits who can pass through walls. The level of spirits is stormy and crowded.

But, says Huston Smith, moving up to the highest level is like the moment your climbing airplane clears the storm clouds. The weather is so calm, the sun shines so brightly, and the clouds that a minute ago shook your airliner now look like a fluffy carpet. Religion teaches that higher is better. Things in our world that seemed so difficult are put into perspective. Combat in the spirit world between Gaia and Poseidon, when seen from the higher level, is simply the natural interaction of earth and sea. When we learn to "look at your life with heaven's eyes," to quote the wise priest in *Prince of Egypt*, we become wiser, more objective. We develop the Dalai Lama's key virtue: compassion.

Typically, religions describe one more circle, the biggest one humans can imagine, the red one. Dark Matter and Black Holes are the big dimensions of this sphere, and quarks and strings are the tiny dimensions. We give names to the most amazing powers of all, even if we do not understand them: The Creator, The Trinity, The Dao, Nirvana, and Brahman. When higher powers come down to our level, we call it 'revelation.' This word means "unveiling."

Christians believe that the character of God is most fully visible in Jesus. Aquinas said, "the slenderest knowledge of higher things is worth more to a person than the most certain knowledge of lesser things."

Hindus worship Krishna because he came down the ladder of being to bring higher knowledge to the lower places.

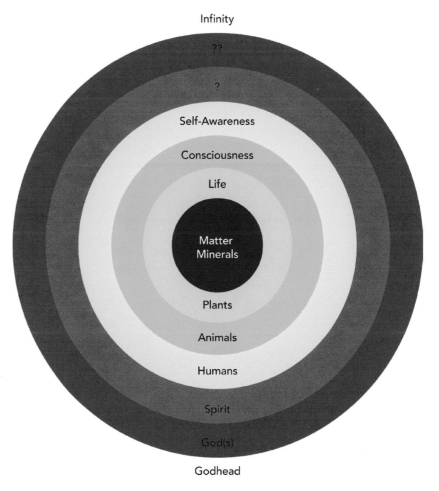

TRADITIONAL WORLDVIEW

Infinity

??

?

Self-Awareness

Consciousness

Life

Matter
Minerals

Plants

Animals

Humans

Spirit

God(s)

Godhead

Jews follow the commandments of Moses because they came from the mountaintop. Aquinas said, "the slenderest knowledge of higher things is worth more to a person than the most certain knowledge of lesser things."

The Qur'an, for Muslims, is more like Jesus for Christians: the actual word of God come down to earth. Muslims say that Jesus and Muhammad were prophets, but not incarnations of God.

The great prophets speak in symbols: "bread of life," "forbidden fruit," "judgment day." Interpreting those symbols is the job of scripture. But remember: symbols mean more than one thing simultaneously. They come from intuition, not logic. For example, does "lamb of God" mean that Jesus was a sheep? No, it means he was gentle. And loved by God. And a sacrificial victim of human sin. And one of the chosen people. And probably hundreds of other things that only poets and artists could think of.

But that is not the end. It's just the end of our knowledge. There are 100 beads on a Muslim rosary. Ninety-nine have divine names. The last bead stands for the un-nameable. St. Paul called it "the peace that surpasses all understanding." Utter mystery. Huston Smith summed it up like this: the world we know is surrounded by a fascinating, mysterious darkness. Compared to the infinite, we are like a protein in a cell on a human finger. The protein cannot know the cell. How then can it imagine, let alone understand, the skin, the muscle, the knuckles, and so on, much less the whole hand? And even if it could contain all that understanding, it could never imagine the hand fingering a guitar, the fist clenching in anger, or the delicate touch of a surgeon repairing a heart. It's just a little protein! That's how small we are, so low on the ladder of reality, compared to the Infinite. We are born and we die in mystery, but the mystery fascinates us.

Unlike the protein cell, we *know* there is something greater. It's why we study religion: we know that although we are very small, we need to know about these great things:

- Reality is Infinite
- Reality has an order, from higher to lower
- The lower things depend on the higher
- The higher we look, the more unified and great things become
- With our powers of consciousness and self-awareness, we can't help but ask:

What's above us?

Where do we fit?

How did we get here?

Where are we going?

How shall we live?

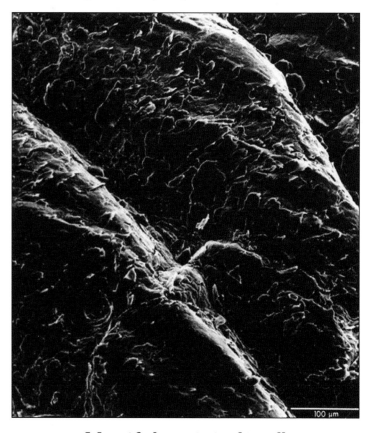

Magnified protein in skin cell

CHAPTER 3

What do we know, and how do we know it?

Since we know things using our brains, everything we know is subjective. But some things seem more certain than others. More scientific. Proven.

Here is an allegory about science and knowing, as told by Huston Smith. Picture a girl walking down a path at night. In her hand is a flashlight. When she shines it downward on the path, it lets her see tree roots, rocks, a little frog, and the bends in the path.

When she hears someone up ahead, she pulls the beam up to horizontal, and gets a glimpse of the person approaching. As her friend comes near, she sees who it is, but not much more. She can't see her friend's ideas, or the story she is about to tell. The really interesting things are hidden from our traveler and her flashlight.

Now suppose they begin walking together. The girl with the flashlight aims it at the stars to show her which one is the Big Dipper and, of course, they begin laughing. The flashlight is useless.

In an allegory, everything stands for something else: the path is like the journey through life. The night is the mysteriousness of the universe. The flashlight is science and its beam is observation, experimentation, and understanding. The girls are people like us, trying to see their way through life.

When the girls in the forest try to understand something below their level, they are like a person shining their flashlight down. Science can tell us a lot about plants or the little frog. When they look one another, the flashlight reveals what's outside, but not what's inside. And what's inside us is much more important than what's visible, right? Aren't your memories, plans, and feelings more important than your eye color or the way you cut your hair? And then, to illuminate the things above our level, like angels or God, symbolized by the stars? Science is useless. If there were angels, science couldn't prove it. If there is a God, no experiment could reveal it. Experiments require a control as well as a variable. By definition, higher powers are beyond our control.

But so much of what we know is true *really is true*, thanks to science. Gravity is not just an opinion. We can prove things our senses detect, things below our level. We "know" higher powers by intuition, by faith, by insight. Such things are the stuff of religion, music, and art.

In between the high and the low are the things on our level. We use both kinds of knowing (scientific proof AND plain old trust) to find the truth. In history or psychology we describe the appearance and activities of people as accurately as we can. And we do our best to understand our inner worlds. In short, we know the truth about each other by proof AND trust.

	Allegory	**Method/s**	**Examples**
Above	*Flashlight of scientific knowledge useless to illuminate the sky*	*We know by trust.*	*"I know there is a God, because people I respect tell me so."* (faith in God with no direct experience) *"God is true: I feel his presence in nature and music and when I do good deeds."* (faith in God with some emotional experience)
Our own level	*Flashlight useful in seeing the outside of other people. Most important truths about others we cannot 'see' except by intuition and experience.*	*We know by part trust, part proof.*	*"I can tell you are worried—what's it all about?"* (explaining your moods and reasons is very subjective) *"Tell me what happened next. I can't believe it!"* (eyewitness accounts are sometimes unreliable) *"I know he's guilty. The jury said so."* (the authority has decreed that it's true.) *"I know you are happy because I see your smile."* (appearances can usually be trusted)
Below	*Flashlight is useful in seeing everything in the path. Use of scientific method*	*We know by proof.*	*"I know J.K. Rowling wrote Harry Potter."* (all evidence points to it) *"I know baseball will begin in April"* (you can rely on it happening as scheduled) *"I know the letter P comes after J in the alphabet."* (everyone agrees on the order of letters) *"I know that 2 + 2 = 4."* (by logical proof)

CHAPTER 4

Theisms and Atheisms

Our religion is sometimes like being Korean or French: we were born into a tradition and raised to do and believe certain things. We don't think about them too much, and may even believe that analyzing or criticizing a religious faith is disrespectful and could lead to loss of faith.

But the purpose of this course is to develop a deeper understanding of ones' own faith—and doubt—by looking at the faith of others. Since the Enlightenment in the West, Christians and Jews in particular have scrutinized the supernatural side of religion. This chapter is written in that spirit, to make you think at a more mature level than you did as a child. Why do you think there is no God? Why do you wish there was a God? Why do you trust there is a God? What good reasons do you have for thinking as you do? What childhood beliefs are you keeping and which ones are you discarding?

THEISMS

In our age, people are likely to dismiss any supernatural beliefs, including the belief in a Higher Power like God. Science has become our most trusted way of knowing. As we saw in the last two chapters, however, the power of science lies in its self-discipline. If those levels of being in the diagram on page 13 are real, they're beyond proving and disproving, so science can't tell us much, at least not yet.

But this limitation does not stop us from developing explanations about what Huston Smith calls "The One, The Many, The More." Here are three:

I. Anselm's explanation of the existence of "TWNGCBC"

- The word "God" means "That Which Nothing Greater Can Be Conceived" (TWNGCBC), the most perfect being.
- The word "Perfect" means "as really itself as possible." Nowadays, it means more things, but that's the original meaning.
- Now think of a perfect sandwich, the perfect murder, the perfect friend, the perfect day: wouldn't each one be more perfect if it was real, and not just an idea?
- A God which exists only in the mind is less perfect than a real God would be.
- Since "God" refers to *the* most perfect being, then God must exist in reality, not only in someone's mind. By definition, God is greater than the mind thinking about God. Joseph Campbell wrote: "God is a metaphor for the mystery that absolutely transcends all human categories of thought, even the categories of being and non-being."

II. Thomas Aquinas' explanation of the UCFC

1. Every event in the world is caused by some event that happened before.
2. Either (a) the series of causes is infinite, or
3. (b) the series of causes goes back to a first cause, which has no cause.
4. But an infinite series of causes is impossible.
5. Therefore, a first cause, which one could call "God," must have existed. It had to start somewhere! God is the Uncaused First Cause (UCFC).

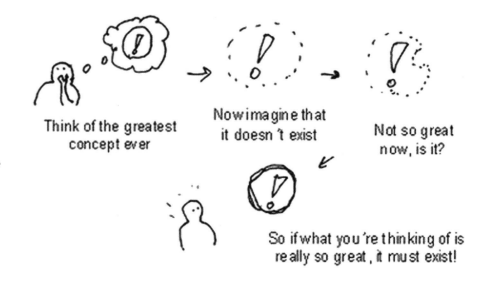

Think of the greatest concept ever

Now imagine that it doesn't exist

Not so great now, is it?

So if what you're thinking of is really so great, it must exist!

III. E.F. Schumacher's "Progressions" explanation

The known universe contains at least four levels of being, each with a unique power which makes it more complex than the level(s) below. You will, I hope, remember this Great Chain of Being from Chapter Two.

- Highest known level: M + x + y + z, the level of humans. We exist (M), are alive (x), have consciousness (y), and the higher power of self-awareness (z)
- M + x + y, the level of animals. Existence (m), plus life (x), plus the higher power of consciousness (y)
- M + x, the level of plants. They have existence (M), and the higher power of life (x)
- Lowest level: M, matter. It has the power of existence.

Progressing up the chain of being, things get more complex, more creative, more free, more self-determined, and have more spiritual life than the levels below.

But, on a scale of zero to 100%, moving upwards, we are nowhere near the top. Humans are far from being 100% complex, 100% creative, 100% free, 100% self-determined, or 100% spiritual. There must be at least one level—maybe a lot more—higher than ourselves. If there's nothing up there, what a waste of space!

Such a higher level could be called "God" or something similar. C.S. Lewis compares God to the Sun: "I believe in Christianity as I believe that the Sun has risen: not only because I see it, but because by it, I see everything else."

ATHEISMS

With the Renaissance, Reformation, and Enlightenment in Europe, Christianity was challenged again and again to change itself. Atheism became a reasonable and popular option as the church lost its grip on most of the institutions of Europe. Socrates had long ago shown that you don't need religion to be ethical. Science was showing that religious explanations of astronomy, biology, and geology, just to name a few, were far inferior to what scientists were able to measure and demonstrate by experiment. Atheism, once a crime, became a valid answer to many paradoxes. Here are four famous arguments in favor of atheism.

A. Either God is all-knowing OR We are free, but not both. If God is omniscient, then does God know the future? If so, then he knows what we are going to do, and so we aren't really free: we are GOING to marry that person, or quit that job, or catch that virus. If God does NOT know the future, then God is not omniscient. So which is it?

B. Nothing, not even God, can be omnipotent. Omnipotent means "can do everything," right? OK, so can God make a rock so heavy that God can't lift it? No? Then there is something God can't do (make the rock). Yes? Then there is still something God can't do (lift the rock). Hmmmmm.

C. God's all good? Really? Then why create the devil or send people ETERNALLY to hell? How could an all-good being let loose such a force of evil or commit such an act of damnation?

D. The Idea of "God" makes no sense. Epicurus, the Greek philosopher, once asked:

Q: Is God willing to prevent evil, but not able?
A: *Then he is not omnipotent.*
Q: Is he able to, but not willing?
A: *Then he is cruel.*
Q: Is he both able, and willing?
A: *Then where does evil come from?*
Q: Is he neither able nor willing?
A: *Then why call him God?*

GOD: AN INVENTION OR A DISCOVERY?

Human beings have invented plenty of things, including the alphabet you and I are now using. The Bible was written by people. Cathedrals and Temples are is man-made. But religious people insist that they found God, or God found them. They aren't praying to an imaginary friend they made up but to the actual source of all goodness who communicates with us and wants us to love one another as He has loved us.

God is real, they say, revealed to people through the natural world, dreams, inspiration, art, and music. Being "made in the image of God" makes us tiny but real reflections of the invisible world of the spirit, so looking inside ourselves is also a way of spiritual discovery.

Others say that religion is a story people made up so they would worry less about the unknown. Invented, like Santa Claus: a nice story, but fiction. What do you think? How much of religion is invented and how much discovered?

Many of us are religious for the same reason we are Korean or French: we were born into a tradition and raised to do and believe certain things. We don't think about them too much, and may even believe that analyzing or criticizing a religious faith is disrespectful and could lead to loss of faith.

But religion isn't God. There's no doubt that religion is invented, but God could be a discovery. The purpose of this course is to develop a deeper understanding of ones' own faith—and doubt—by looking at the faith of others. Since the Enlightenment in the West, Christians and Jews in particular have scrutinized the supernatural side of religion. This chapter was written in that spirit, to make you think at a more mature level than you did as a child. Why do you think there is no God? Why do you wish there was a God? Why do you trust there is a God? What good reasons do you have for thinking as you do? What childhood beliefs are you keeping and which ones are you discarding?

CHAPTER 5

Defining Religion

Once upon a time, there were six blind men living in a small town in India. They were friends, and they loved good discussions. When a commotion outside their temple distracted them, they asked a little boy what the matter was. He told them, with delight in his voice, "someone has brought an elephant into the courtyard!"

Now since they had been blind since birth, the six had never seen an elephant, but they had heard of it.

"It is as tall as a house!" said one. "It is heavier than any living thing," said another." A third said, "elephants are very intelligent." "Well," the fourth one announced, "I am going to see for myself." They all laughed, because blind people can't "see," but when he returned, smiling from ear to ear, he said, "the elephant keeper let me touch the elephant, and I am here to tell you: it is not big at all! It is like a snake hanging down from a tree." (He had only grasped the elephant's tail).

The fifth man said he was going "for a look," and they all laughed again, and when he came back, he declared that the elephant was more like the trunk of a tree. (He had been brought to the elephant's leg). The sixth man did the same, and pronounced HIS verdict: like a shirt flapping on a clothesline (it was the ear). And the first three took their turns arguing that the elephant was like a spear (the tusk) or a wall (the side) or a hose (the elephant had squirted water at him from her trunk). The discussion kept up for quite some time about something they all claimed to understand, but none of them had seen. Everybody has a theory about the mysteries of the universe. None of us has really seen the answer. The elephant is the symbol for God.

Here are five definitions of religions, each probably as imperfect as the blind men's definitions. After seeing their mistake about the elephant, it would be smart to start with a definition about how hard it is to really know God.

Definition One: "Religion is the story we tell about the unseen, the biggest dimensions of the universe and the tiniest ones inside the human mind."

Definition Two: Here's Webster's Dictionary:
1. "The belief in a god or group of gods," or
2. "An organized system of beliefs, ceremonies, and rules used to worship a god or group of gods."

OK, but that leaves Buddhism out. They teach that everyone can have their own god-beliefs or none at all. Is the fourth-largest religion in the world not a religion because many of them don't believe in a supernatural being?

We're not totally sure where the word "religion" comes from, but one possible place is with two Latin words, re (meaning do it again) and ligare (meaning tie together). Religamenting. Binding together. Religion is the way we put back together what has fallen apart. That would bring Buddhism back, because the practice of finding the Buddha-nature is religious. You are connecting back together the strands that weave a good life.

Definition Three: "Religion is the human outreach to re-connect with the One, the Many, the More."

How many people does it take to make a religion? Do they have to have a creed, a prophet, a holy book, or a ritual? Is it possible for everyone to have their own religion? Do we want to exclude individualists? The ones who blaze their own paths?

Definition Four: "Religion is a person's way of answering life's questions that can only be answered by trust." (Thanks to The Rev. Randy Sherren for this definition.)

Religion is not about questions that science can handle best, like why the sum of the angles in a triangle always adds up to 180 degrees. It doesn't get into things we can answer using our five senses: like 'what time is it?' or 'what is the capital of Sri Lanka?' or 'does that apple taste sweet or tart?' Religion is saved for the questions that involve trust. Faith. Knowing without scientific proof. That's not so unusual. We use trust all the time, like when we expect

His holiness, the fourtheenth Dalai Lama

people to keep promises or follow directions on the label. We trust that the sun will come up tomorrow: would anyone want to bet me that it won't? I trust that my wife loves me, although I can't prove it. I trust that the clock on my phone is accurate.

Trust is not an *inferior* way to know things.

Here are some of life's questions that can *only* be answered by trust,

"Is the universe random, or is there a Plan?"
"Are we here for a reason?"
"If there is a God, is he/she all good? Why/why not?"
"How did we get here?" and
"How should I live?"

Definition Five: "If it's based on compassion, it's worthy of the name 'religion.'" Some cults and self-centered beliefs don't qualify. This definition is by His Holiness the Dalai Lama.

Definitions tell us what we're going to study, what we're going to leave out, and why. What do *you* think religion is?

CHAPTER 6

Comparing Religions

How can we compare one religion with another?

Of course, you could just say, "my religion is best, and the closer a religion is to mine, the better it is." But what makes you so sure? Or you could say, "all religions are equally true, or equally wrong, or equally valuable," but again, how do you know? Ninian Smart offered an answer to this question. He thought it was wiser to just compare religions using seven dimensions.

- **Myth:** what sacred stories do they tell to interpret the universe and humans' place in it?
- **Ritual:** what ceremonies celebrate and dramatize the myths and narratives?
- **Experience:** what do people go through? How do they try to repeat the actions of the founder/s?
- **Institutions:** what makes someone a member of the group, and what attitudes and activities do they share?
- **Ethics:** what rules of behavior do they follow?
- **Doctrines:** what is their basic system of beliefs?
- **Objects and places:** material symbols of the sacred.

As you study the religions in this book, you might keep track of them in terms of these seven dimensions. We may not cover all seven aspects of every religion, but we have found these categories to be very useful in comparing one to another.

Chapter 7

Indigenous Religions

VIDEO 1. MANOOMIN, THE SACRED FOOD

https://vimeo.com/58824154

As you saw in the video, the Anishinabe have a Sky God who sent a messenger to the people and pointed them west, to Minnesota. They would find food growing on top of the water, and they did: wild rice is now sacred to them. The idea of genetically-modifying most crops is fine, they say, but not the few sacred things like wild rice. Sacred means "set apart." There are different rules for sacred things and places, which draw our attention higher.

VIDEO 2. MBUTI, CHILDREN OF THE FOREST
https://vimeo.com/65184596

The Mbuti are classic examples of Stage One religion. The Sky God made the forest and oversees everything, but the forest itself cares for them, not the Sky God. One could say that the forest is a Stage Two Goddess, except that rather than being separate from her people, like a goddess would be, the forest is a complex organism: plants, animals, and people.

VIDEO 3. AUSTRALIAN ABORIGINAL DREAMING VIDEO

https://youtu.be/gYgdBRCb88o

"Dreamtime" is what we might call "Eternity." It's "once upon a time," outside of the usual time and space. Australian Aborigines call it The Dreaming because they understand our dreams as symbolic windows into the spiritual dimension of eternity. When the ancestor animals

"sang" Australia's land and creatures into existence, that time and place was The Dreaming. It always was, always is, and always will be. In dreamtime, they walked across the continent, following "songlines," making red mountains or poisonous snakes. These ancestor animals hid water under the desert, and the songlines told future singers where to find it. Therefore, a big part of their religion is learning the songs. The Dreaming was not fully-understood by creatures lower than humans, who only wanted to understood their own limited worlds. But man and woman walked across the land and understood all the dimensions. The Dreaming is Now, and Then, and Someday.

VIDEO 4. THE TWO WORLDS OF THE BAKONGO:

https://www.youtube.com/watch?v=H9iy5TTALBQ

My Haverford College professor, Wyatt MacGaffey first got me exploring the religions of the world. He did his fieldwork as an anthropologist in the forest of the Lower Congo River in Africa. He taught us that we needed to put aside the "lenses" we used to see the world and learn to see through the lenses made by symbolic stories (myths) and dramas (rituals).

In one ritual, a hunter consulted an *nganga*, an expert in connecting with the spirit world. The *nganga* had the hunter sacrifice a chicken to feed the soul of a spirit called "Makwende," symbolized by a Power Figure or *nkisi*, such as you saw in the video. The spirit Makwende took the shape of a leopard in the spirit world, and accepted the soul of the chicken as payment for an errand: go find the spirit who is blocking the hunter's gun and kill him. After the chicken sacrifice, the *nganga* told the hunter to go try again, and to have faith. Sure enough, his good luck returned. He aimed at a deer, and brought it down to feed his family. The sacrifice is based on a two-world theory. Our world is the land of the living. The other world, where Makwende can roam, is the land of the dead. Each world is the opposite of the other. Here, people are normal-looking, have black skin, and are awake during the day. There, people are ghostly-looking, with white skin, and are awake during the night. They have houses and families. They live a whole lifetime over there, and when they die, they are reincarnated into THIS world again.

In other words, it's one reincarnation after another, with no end. When we live in the land of the dead, we have more power and can haunt or help those we left behind in the land of the living. God lives far away, and is pretty much the Sky God. It's the spirits, such as the one symbolized by the *nkisi* Power Figure, that get involved. The key to a good life is to keep the ancestors happy, and when they interfere, figure out what we did wrong; and make it up to them, with sacrifices, kind words, or ceremonial gifts.

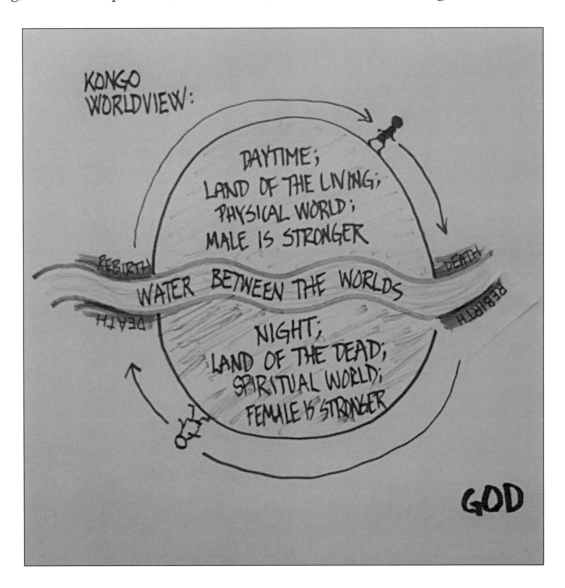

CHAPTER 8

Creation Stories Comparison Project

Now that we're at the end of Unit One, your teacher may choose to have you sum up a few of the Roots of Religion. Here's one idea: Investigate Creation stories from around the world. Report the name of the culture, country, and/or religion that identifies it (extra credit if no one else chooses the one you did) a description of the Creator, whether that's a god or some other being, the reason/problem/crisis/need that caused the Creator to start the process, and the role humans played. A photo, symbol, or diagram and citation go at the end, and then your name.

Submit your poster on-line or make a poster on paper for the bulletin board.

EXAMPLE ONE, FROM GENESIS

Creator	The creator is Yahweh, a being outside time and space.
Reason	He wanted to make the universe out of nothing. God is full of creativity.
Creation Process	Over six days, God made all the dimensions of matter, and time, and all the living things on the planet. The earth sits on pillars with domes holding back the waters of the sky. (See diagram)
Humans	God made humans last, and humans resemble God more than any other animals do. Humans have free will, creativity, the ability to give names to things, and curiosity. After death, we inhabit an underworld called Sheol. God dwells above and beyond, but cares about humans.

THE ANCIENT HEBREW CONCEPTION
OF THE UNIVERSE
TO ILLUSTRATE THE ACCOUNT OF CREATION AND THE FLOOD

EXAMPLE TWO, AN ANISHINABE CREATION STORY

Creator   The creator is called Gitchi Manitou, kind of a Sky God. He dreams about Mother Earth, emotions, the four elements, and all the animals, including us, and wakes up from the dream.

Reason   Gitchi Manitou decides that a real world is better than a dream world, and once things get going, he can stay active by warning humans about upcoming dangers, since Gitchi Manitou, being eternal, can see into the future.

Creation Process   When he wakes up, he decides that his dream ought to be real, and then, through circling motion, creates the circle of life, the circle of the seasons, the four directions, the animals of the water, sky, land, and plants, and then humans.

Humans   Humans are made to be hunters and tenders of plants, and are like Gitchi Manitou: they, too, can dream. When seven prophets come to give them the message to move from the East Coast, they follow the prophets directions until they find the food growing on the water, *manoomin*, wild rice. This was promised by Gitchi Manitou. They settled in the upper midwest of the USA by around 1400.

PART TWO

Polytheistic Religions

By settling in one place, and farming, human groups could be larger. There was enough extra food that people could live in towns, and they guarded their surpluses with weapons and walls. The invention of metal tools and division of labor helped spur population growth, and cities developed, with increasing specialization. Poets composed songs about more and more gods, each in charge of something different, and scribes wrote them down, using the newly invented methods of writing on clay or papyrus. Altars became shrines, and then temples, sometimes rivaling the homes of royalty. Royalty: a great invention for the ones wearing the crown; not so much for those supplying tribute, taxes, soldier-sons, and serving-daughters. Priests often served the rulers, as well. Critics of rulers, such as the prophets of the Hebrew Bible, would come at a later stage.

These polytheistic civilizations left a huge body of sacred and not-so-sacred writings, art, and temples for us to study. In this part, we'll look at Indian, Greek, Norse, Maya, Zoroastrian, and Canaanite religion, finishing with another comparison project on Flood Stories from polytheistic religions all over the globe. We start with three chapters on the most famous, most populous, and maybe oldest polytheistic religion of them all, Hinduism.

CHAPTER 9

Hinduism: Gods

Hinduism is the biggest, most complex, and probably the oldest of the world's religions. But it isn't really a religion. It's like calling all the religions of this continent "Americism." The first one was the polytheistic religion of the Indus (*Hindu* comes from the name) Valley Civilization, around 2500 BCE. They used the lotus position for meditation, the Swastika as a symbol of well-being (how ironic now, thanks to Hitler) and worshipped many gods; but no temples (or palaces) have been found from this era.

Two new gods appeared by 1500, the city-dweller Indra and the god of fire, Agni. An upper class called the "Brahmin caste" was added to the top of the two classes already in place (nobles and commoners). Eventually, the caste system would become very rigid and tied to beliefs about reincarnation. By this point, archaeologists say, temples were being built in many of the cities of the Indus Valley.

HINDU POLYTHEISM AND MONOTHEISM

The Brahmins brought many rituals and epic poems with them. The epics, called "Vedas," present Vishnu the sun-god and Shiva the marauding mountain-god who inspired a fearful loyalty among mortals. Other gods at this early stage included

- **Yama,** the first human, who became divine after death, taking control of death and the underworld.
- The **Devas** and the **Asuras**, groups of gods who often opposed each other. The Asuras would later become demons.
- **Dyeus,** the Chief God or Sky God. You might recognize his name, which became "Dios," "Theos," and "Dieu" in Spanish, Greek, and French.
- **Shiva** (the oldest worshipped Lord in India) and Vishnu, who battled over the whole earth.

By the year 300 BCE, in the great epic *Mahabharata*, the roles of the gods had evolved again. There was now a ruling trinity:

- **Brahma** (taking over from Dyeus), the creator
- **Shiva** / the destroyer / Lord of the Dance
- **Vishnu** the preserver / supreme soul / incarnating savior

By 100 BCE, the idea of the total oneness of the universe, describable and indescribable, was born. This Big Everything is known as Brahman. It is the soul of the universe, and each of us has within us a part of it, called atman. Brahman is Hindu monotheism, including all the gods; indeed, all reality. Brahman was not one being, but All Being.

The gods and goddesses of Hinduism almost all have at least one temple or shrine, and Shiva and Vishnu have by far the most. Temples to Shiva feature statues of the god riding a bull, a symbol of his dangerous power. Vishnu Temples are usually dedicated to one of his incarnations, like Rama, Krishna, or the Buddha. Vishnu has lots of blue and many arms (he's the helpful one, after all). Temples dedicated to Parvati include her role as goddess of power, and the triumph of good over evil. She is also an incarnation of the Mother Goddess Durga, and spouse of Shiva. When Parvati is portrayed next to Shiva, she has just two arms; but on her own, she can have many more.

While Hinduism was and still is polytheistic, most modern Hindus consider themselves monotheistic. How is this possible? Well, Brahman is so big and diverse as to be impossible to relate to. Like air, Brahman is all around and we can't live without it, but who prays to air or sings praise to oxygen? So the other gods are symbols of the relatable natures of Brahman. Just as you are a student, and a son/daughter, and a member of a team or club, so too is God simultaneously Creator, Preserver, and Destroyer. Modern Hindus use these gods like a prism: the pure light of Brahman is made of the many colors of Brahma, Shiva, Vishnu, and all the others.

Hindu Temple, Maple Grove, Minnesota

CHAPTER 10

Hinduism: The Four Wants.

One of the surprising things about these "Hinduisms" is what a long-range view of life they take. These religions teach that a soul travels through thousands of bodies on its journey, going from lifetime to lifetime in a quest for release from the cycle of reincarnations. Judaism, Christianity, and Islam teach that we have only this life. So, let's step back and ask: what are people supposed to get from life, and how can religion help them get it? The Hindu answer is, "people want different things at different stages of their life, and in different lifetimes." The first two wants—both selfish—are called The Path of Desire.

The First Want: we begin by wanting pleasure. Children want fun and happiness; and as little suffering and pain as possible. When we grow up, we don't give up wanting pleasure. You might think of the First Want as the base of a pyramid, underlying all the future, higher wants. There is nothing wrong with this, and each lifetime begins with this stage.

But pretty soon, as Huston Smith describes it in his great book *The World's Religions*, pleasure alone is not enough. It's self-centered, and it's obvious that we are not the center of the world.

The Second Want: we crave success: money, fame, and power. Wanting these things moves us out into the world. As we strive for a good GPA, or a high batting average, or a cool girlfriend, we compete in the marketplace. We win or lose. This is the stage of achievement, of success for our own benefit.

Unfortunately, there are many more losers than winners, and besides, you can't take money with you when you die. Fame is fleeting (Andy Warhol said we should all get 15 minutes of fame. If you don't know who he was, it proves his point). Power is temporary (ask any politician). So we don't give up wanting pleasure and success, but we know there is more.

The third and fourth wants—both unselfish—are called the Path of Letting Go.

The Third Want: we want to serve our world. It leads you to parenthood, to social service, to work for justice and peace in the world, and to unselfish compassion of all kinds. Typically, it involves duty, responsibility, and long-term commitment. If you start a company so you can make a million bucks, that's the Second Want. If you also start the business so as to employ people, help their families, and supply your town with a good product, fairly-made and fairly-priced, that's the Third Want. Most people don't get any farther than this stage, but success in serving the world earns them gratitude.

The Fourth Want. But if you're really honest, after a lifetime of (1) pleasure, (2) success, and (3) doing your community duties, there is still more. Hinduism says it's time to (4) give up everything. Possessions, desires, and even relationships are too much baggage to carry with you. Remember: Hindus say we're on a very, very long journey toward release from the cycle of reincarnations. The more you give up (renounce) the closer you are to release ("moksha").

So, in this optional and very difficult final stage, an older person sells the house, gives his/her money away, and becomes a homeless wanderer. They are poor by choice, relying on the charity of others. They beg, but not for much. They wear the simplest of clothing and eat little. They may sleep outside. But these wanderers know that there is something more to want than they've ever had. The Wanderer gives up all finite things for a chance at the three infinities:

- time without boundaries
- knowledge without limits
- joy without end

It sounds a lot like Heaven, far away and hard to reach. But the teachings of Hinduism say, "not so." Instead of a person living only once, and being judged by an Infinite Being, and going to a place of Infinite Bliss, Hindus say, 'we already have all three infinities. We just don't realize it.'

People only *seem* separate from one another. We have our own soul, called *atman* but those souls are really just our own piece of the one true soul of the universe, Brahman. When we die, our *atmans* leave our temporary bodies and, like drops of rain in a lake, they rejoin the Brahman, the Big Everything.

So, we close with some bad math:

1. Let "B" equal Brahman.
2. B = 1 because "all is one."
3. B = infinity because it includes everything.
4. Therefore 1 = infinity.
5. Hmmm.

CHAPTER 11

Hinduism: Four Stages, Four Castes, Four Paths

Reincarnation is sort of like getting a new car every few years. In my previous life I might have been a doctor, a baker, or a ballerina. I'll never know. Hinduism teaches that a person ought to work hard doing their duty in THIS life, so as to be reincarnated to higher and higher levels until they get released from having to return.

Samsara is the turning cycle of reincarnation. *Moksha* is the moment of being freed from the cycle and joining the eternal Brahman. Hinduism teaches people to break through the limits to joy: pain, frustration, and boredom. They seek wisdom, not just knowledge. And they try to live fully, all the time, as a child of the universe, at one with everything and not alienated from anything.

FOUR STAGES

There are ceremonies to mark your progress through the four stages of life. You might make it to stage 2 in this life, and stage 3 in your next six lives, and then lead a bad life and fall back to the level of an animal or a very low-status, "untouchable" person. Here's a quick summary of the four stages, which match up pretty closely with the Four Wants.

Student Stage: After a playful childhood (First Want), you start your formal religious studies with an initiation ceremony at age 11 to 13. In the traditional system, you would live with your guru (teacher) and study religion, math, literature, languages, and martial arts. Here you make a start at the Second Want (success)

Householder Stage: Then, after the ceremony of (arranged) marriage, you take on the duties of the second stage: family, work, and community. Here, you continue with your pursuit of success, the Second Want.

Retirement Stage: This goes with completing all your striving for success. You have raised your children, made your fortune, become famous, paid off the mortgage, whatever. Now comes the time to learn who you really are, a spiritual being on an earthly journey for a short time. You are tempted in your twilight years to go back to the fun of the First Want, but that isn't going to move you up in the next incarnation. Most end their years serving others (the Third Want). The most serious moksha-seeker, however, goes for the prize.

Wandering Pilgrim Stage: The final stage is only attempted by the few who go after the Fourth Want, which requires giving up everything that attaches you to the finite world. Yep, everything. Possessions and relationships. You find that you need less and less food. Less and less clothing. Wandering pilgrims beg for the few coins they need for food, and these holy homeless ones (called *sannyasins*) are treated with great respect. They are living saints. This might be their very last lifetime before they rejoin the One Soul.

FOUR CASTES

When the Aryans migrated to India long ago, they brought with them a class system now known by a Portugese word, *caste* (pronounced "cast.")
1. The highest classes are the people the closest to moksha: the priests and wise seers, the Brahmins
2. Administrators, soldiers, and organizers, the Kshatriyas
3. Producers, artists, builders, and other craftspeople, the Vaishyas
4. Followers: workers of many kinds, the Shudras

When you die, if you did the duties of your caste, you may move up a level. If you ignored your duty (the word for duty is "dharma") or went against it, you would move down in your next life. So no one is permanently upper or lower class. You move, but only between lives.

There are also people so low in status and so wretched in their existence that they are called "untouchables." They have sinned so much in a previous life that they returned in this almost sub-human state as punishment. It's like hell, and it lasts a lifetime, but that's a lot shorter than eternal damnation, isn't it? Mohandas Gandhi, the founder of the modern Indian republic, taught that untouchability was cruel, and renamed these sub-caste people harijans, meaning "children of God." Untouchability is now illegal, and slowly dying out.

Gandhi made untouchability illegal

If you do your dharma as determined by your caste and your stage, you will get good karma attached to your atman like a positive electrical charge. Failure to do your dharma results in negative karma. When you die, no god judges you. The weight of your soul and the level of its karma automatically transfers it into its next mother's womb. A new human is created and the Brahman delivers your atman.

FOUR PATHS

We've looked at the four wants, the four stages, and the four castes. The "fourth four" completes the set, and refers to how each individual person can best do their dharma, regardless of their want, stage or caste. Everyone has their own personality, and in the ancient scripture *Bhagavad Gita*, Lord Krishna told Arjuna that there are four main types. The Ancient Greeks said almost the same thing. For each personality type is a "yoga" religious style that works best for them.

Karma Yoga: The first path is for the person who prefers action. They don't want to read a lot of books or meditate for long periods in the lotus position. They feel fulfilled by serving in a soup kitchen, building a school, or teaching an immigrant to read. They respect people who do their duty even when it is very difficult. If you choose this path, your teacher or guru will instruct you through a series of tasks and responsibilities. The older you get, the more you will need to do to help others. The toughest thing about this path is detachment. You don't do your duty to get praise, or rewards, or fame. You do the right thing, you do your best, and let the outcome happen. Don't think about what you might get from doing good. In fact, if your deeds are not noticed, that is probably better for you. The archer Arjuna balked at doing his duty when he realized that going into battle would mean killing some of his cousins in the enemy army. But Lord Krishna, an incarnation of the god Vishnu, told him this: in every lifetime, we get a specific duty to do. Arjuna can't see the greater purpose served by fighting and maybe killing a relative. But from the perspective of eternity, Krishna tells him, this is his small role to play during this life.

Jnana Yoga: The second path is for the person with an intellectual curiosity about the world and its eternal meanings. Jnana Yoga has four skills which a person develops as they move toward higher consciousness.

- One, knowing the difference between the real (Brahman) and the unreal (mere appearances).
- Two, letting go of attachment to everything that isn't eternal.
- Three, living virtuously: with self-control, faith, endurance, focus on duty, and concentration.
- Four, longing deeply for eternity.

A person on the Jnana Path should not live in their head, however. They must not become dreamy thinkers or idle philosophers. They learn from their teachers to USE their intellect in order to get past all the roadblocks that material, temporary illusions represent. This path involves transcending the self, and seeing with the eyes of the eternal Brahman.

Bhakti Yoga: The Third Path, also explained to Arjuna on that famous battlefield by Lord Krishna, is the path of loving devotion to a personal God. In the first two paths, God is more impersonal, a force or power. Bhakti Yoga is the path of feeling and relationship, and so, it has a lot in common with Judaism and Christianity. You relate to God as your beloved. Or a best friend. Or a loving parent. Or a benevolent master. Krishna, the famous avatar of Vishnu, told his disciples,

> You can only understand Me as I am, as the Personal image of God, by
>
> loving me, dedicating yourself to My work, worshipping Me, and becoming
>
> completely absorbed in Me. Thus will you enter the kingdom of God.
>
> (Bhagavad-Gita, 9.34 & 18.55)

How to do this? Sing. Dance. Worship. Serve (just like Karma Yoga). Contemplate a holy painting. Make a pilgrimage. Devote yourself to seeing God in others. Try to become so close to the One you love that you lose track of the separation between you. This is a good thing, because (remember?) separation is not real anyway.

Raja Yoga: The Fourth Path is what most Americans think of when we hear "Yoga." The word is related to "yoke," the device farmers use to harness the power of animals in plowing or pulling heavy loads. It's a metaphor for self-discipline, harnessing our bodies' animal energy through the use of the mind. Raja Yoga uses many kinds of mind/body work to develop a person's self-control and to bring them closer to a state of patient, quiet alertness. Some of the work involves chanting the syllable OM, which is the sound of creation. All the famous positions of yoga, named after the way different animals carry themselves, help with this quest for Mind over Matter. Flexibility is a key by-product of these positions, but the point is not so much fitness as control. Yogis who walk on coals or fast for long periods are engaging in raja yoga experiments.

CHAPTER 12

The Greek Pantheon

The ancient Greeks described creation like this: at first there was only Chaos, the god of disorder and void. Then Uranus (Father Sky) and Gaia (Mother Earth) began the universe. Their children were the Titans, and the children of the Titans, led by Zeus, overthrew their parents. From that time onwards, these gods ruled Mount Olympus. *Pantheon* means the collection of all the gods in one religion. It's also the name of a temple dedicated to all the gods, not just one. Greece is maybe the best-known Polytheistic (Stage Three) religion. How many gods and goddesses can you identify?

Poseidon	
Hades	
Hestia	
Zeus	
Hera	
Demeter	
Niké	

OK, how about these famous children of Zeus and Hera...

Ares	
Hephaestus	
Apolla	
Aphrodite	
Hermes	
Athena	
Dionysus	
Herakles	

The Greeks believed that the gods had very busy lives in a dimension parallel to ours, and we ought to stay out of the gods' way. Zeus was the High God: not perfect, but superior to the others. As would Thor and Baal in other cultures, Zeus ruled thunder and lightning. They also believed in an impersonal fate, which even the gods had to obey. Humans lived after death in Hades, unless they lost their way there, in which case they were doomed to wander and suffer. In later years, a bad after-world (Tartarus) and a good one (Elysium) began to appear.

Religion in ancient Greece revolved around story (myths) and ritual (Temple sacrifices) designed to train people to avoid *hubris*, that Greek idea of sin as dishonoring yourself. The gods accepted burnt and bloody offerings from earthly altars and would assist the mortals who made them. Hymns, prayers, and dance would accompany these ceremonies. Drama grew from these early myths and rituals. When we come to Socrates, later in the course, we'll see religion turned into philosophy, with less interest in the gods' adventures and more focus on living a good life in this world.

CHAPTER 13

Norse Gods and Goddesses

Norse refers to Scandinavia and the rest of northern Europe. In the beginning, there was nothing. Well, almost nothing: there was a frozen wasteland called Niflheim and a burning place called Muspelheim. When a bit of southern fire and a glacier of northern ice met in the desolate canyon between then, called Ginnungagap, the hideous jotun (giant) named Ymir (see drawing) appeared. From his side a cow was born, and he and the cow for centuries were the only living beings. But one time Ymir fell asleep, and during his hibernation two jotuns—a male and a female—were born. From his left armpit. A six-headed troll grew from his smelly feet. Um, yeah.

That's how the Norse Creation story begins. The Norse people came from somewhere to the east, and brought with them their Aesir or spirits. As with many creation stories, this one spells out the opposites like cold north/hot south, and depicts the first birth in a very unusual way: here, from an armpit and feet; and in the Bible from a man's rib.

Ymir unwillingly provided the stuff from which planet earth was made: some gods killed him. From Ymir's flesh came land and from his blood came the seas. Newer jotuns grew from the earth, including the parents of Odin, who became the one-eyed god of wisdom, war, and death. One poem tells of Odin later being killed by a wolf at Ragnarok, the battle that ends this world. In another poem or "saga," he hangs himself as a sacrifice to himself on the Yggdrasil, the World-Tree, in order to discover the magic that will allow him to control the nine worlds of the universe. Odin has a huge house called Valhalla in Asgard (Heaven). There he gathers the mightiest fallen warriors to form an army that will one day fight at Ragnarok. His most famous son is the thunder-god Thor, with his hammer. "Thursday" is named for him. In fact, four of the seven English names for days of the week are Norse:

Sunday — named after the Sun
Monday — named after the moon
Tuesday — named after Tyr or Tiwas, the Norse sky-god
Wednesday — named after Odin or Wodn, after the Norse chief god
Thursday — named after Thor, the Norse thunder-god
Friday — named after Freya, the warlike goddess of magic, gold, fertility, and love
Saturday — named after the Roman god Saturn

The stories of Norse gods are full of sex, violence, magic, and adventure, and were told for hundreds of years before being written down in the Norse Sagas. Even when Christianity arrived in the northern countries in the 1100s, it adopted customs like the midwinter Yule log and mistletoe for kissing.

CHAPTER 14

Maya Polytheism

Even though their empire of city-states in Central America fell from glory more than a thousand years ago, the Maya people and their stories are still very much alive. Forty percent of the citizens of Guatemala are Maya. Here are a half-dozen of the main gods:

- Several **Sky Gods**, including one for the sun, one for the moon, and others for the planets.
- A **Creator God**, the High God Itzamna. Much later, he was joined by the **Great Feathered Serpent**, a messenger between the gods and the earthly king.
- Gods for rain, lightning, thunder, oceans, and the underworld.
- Several different **Maize Gods**, who get involved not just in growing corn, but many ceremonies that require corn in the rituals. The dwarf shown in the photo of a sculpture from c. 550-800 CE was a human helper of a Maize God in the creation of the world.
- Gods for the hunt, for sex and marriage, childbirth, the hunt (usually a jaguar), and trade.

In the beginning, the Great Feathered Serpent and the High God created the earth, plants, and animals. They noticed that these creatures did not praise them, so they tried to make people, first from mud and later from wood. They failed, but succeeded with corn, which is the most important food crop in the Americas.

These images of the gods described in *Popul Vuh*, a remarkable Mayan scripture, were taken from painted stucco on the sides of pyramids, altars, and pillars in the forests of Central America.

Here's a story from the sixteenth century, called the Hero Twins. It's about life and death, gods and humans, and sports.

Once upon a time there lived twin brothers who wanted to be good farmers, but even the rabbit who stole their crops knew they were not. They were, however, excellent ball-players. The crowds cheered so loudly when they played that they drew the attention of the Lords of Death. They lived in the Underworld, and liked to trick people into dying, especially those who bothered them, like these brothers. So they sent an invitation to the twins to come play a ball game in the Underworld, which the brothers were too frightened to refuse. They prepared as best they could, and set off.

They made it safely across the river of spikes. And the river of blood. And the river of pus. They came at last to the house of the Lords of Death. One of the Lords stood waiting for their greeting, but when the boys said hello, the other Lords rushed out from hiding to show the boys that the first Lord was just a wooden statue. "Did you think our heads are filled with wood?" the Lords cried. The twins had failed a test. "But wait," interrupted one of the Lords," "they did cross all three rivers safely."

The others agreed. "Hardly anyone has ever done that." "Have a seat while we think about what to do with you," one said to the twins. They did, but the bench was burning hot. The boys had failed another test. Then, sent to the Razor House, they escaped by imitating rats, crawling under the sharp blades. Then, in the Jaguar House, they got out alive by feeding bones to the predators. The boys knew, however, that the tests would continue until they died. They lost hope. "Let's see if you can jump over these ovens," smiled one Lord. They jumped straight in, to end their terror and misery. The

Lords of Death tossed the boys' ashes into a river, which you might think was the end of the story. But the Hero Twins discovered something very odd...they were still alive! They were now catfish, swimming about in the river. "I guess we picked up some magic somewhere," said one. And just as he said that, they turned back into their human selves! They soon discovered they had other magical powers. They could cut themselves up and put themselves back together again. They could burn a house down and then restore it. They began to travel from town to town, singing, dancing, and performing fabulous tricks for a living.

The Lord of Death soon heard of their amazing act, and invited them to visit, not realizing these were the very twins they had so recently burned up. When they performed their act, the Lord were delighted. "Do me next!" said one, "Chop me up and put me back together!" The twins were delighted to chop up the Lord. But they did not put him back together. The other Lords, fearing another defeat, sent the twins back to earth. Meanwhile, the gods of the heavens, who had secretly provided a great deal of the twins' magic, honored their courage and cleverness by bringing them up to the sky. One became the Sun and the other the Moon. And their children became rulers of the earth, and build ball courts in every town to honor their ancestors, the Hero Twins.

There are other stories about the first human beings, as in many religions, who, when killed, turned into constellations, invented the 365-day calendar, and taught later people how to write the 20 different names for days. The Maya built cities in the jungle of Central America from about 100 to 900 CE, but abandoned their cities and became village-dwelling farmers. At their peak in around 500 CE, they were intensively farming, building gigantic stone temples covered with brightly-colored murals, writing, and doing math. I took this picture at Tikal, in Guatemala, in the summer of 2013. The stone pillars in front of the pyramid are called "stelae," and each commemorate a birth, crowning, or death of a Maya ruler.

A small temple and stelae in Tikal, Guatemala.

CHAPTER 15

Zoroastrian Dualism

From Iran (Persia) came the teachings of a man named Zoroaster (sometimes known as Zarathustra) and his followers. He lived 600 years BC, about the same time as the Buddha, Kong Fuzi, and Laozi. Zarathustra was the son of a country priest, and had a powerful spiritual vision as a young man of about 30, in which an angel named Good Thought told him that there was just one god, the Wise Lord (Ahura Mazda), not many. To us, this is not that exciting, but in those days, much of religion was about finding the right god for the right situation, and then doing the right sacrifice on the right day, and so on.

Zarathustra taught what could be called "Dualism," instead of pure monotheism, because the Wise Lord had a counterpart, The Evil One. The Wise Lord had twin son-spirits, each free to choose kindness or hostility. One chose hostility and destruction. The other twin chose kindness, and the battle was on. So human beings, who are descended from those two son-spirits, have to choose, also...

> Goodness or Evil?
> Truth or Falsehood?
> Life or Oblivion?
> Enlightenment or Darkness?

And after death, their soul must walk across the Bridge of the Separator, set above the fires of hell, to get to the House of Best Purpose (heaven). The ones who have chosen wrong in life are pushed off the bridge. The rest are saved and are rejoined with their guardian angels.

Zoroastrian priest in fire-temple.

Together, the soul and the angel fight in the great battle against The Evil One.

He also taught that a messiah would come at the end of time and declare a Day of Judgment, at which time their bodies would be resurrected to rejoin their souls. This resurrection is universal, meaning that everyone who has ever lived finally goes to Paradise because good will win the battle with evil. It's possible that his followers taught this idea to Jewish rabbis, or that he learned it from the Jews, since both religions began believing in resurrection around the same time.

Like the Buddha, Zoroaster declared the caste system unjust and refused to allow religion to support it.

Zoroastrians pray five times a day (like Muslims, who came 1200 years after Zoroaster), and give to charity. Like the Bible, their Avesta is a collection of sacred texts gathered over 1000 years. A fire always burns in their temples, and sandalwood makes the smoke smell sweet. Zoroaster's rules for living are still admirable: "Doing good for others is not a duty. It is a joy." "Treasure the love you receive more than anything else. It will last longer than health or wealth." and "You should always be good to strangers. You never know when you will be a stranger yourself."

They neither bury nor cremate their dead, but leave them atop a sacred tower, where the birds of the air take their flesh.

The Kaaba of Zoraster

The remaining bones are kept in a shared central well to await resurrection. They live in the House of Best Purpose (heaven) or the House of Worst Existence (hell), depending on what they chose. Zoroastrian ideas about the afterlife seem to be closely related to the religions of Abraham (see Part Four).

Zoroastrians number perhaps 150,000 worldwide, with significant numbers only in India, the USA, and Central Asia. Their birth rate is small, and their average age quite old, so the religion which once dominated a large part of Southwest Asia may be in danger of extinction.

CHAPTER 16

Canaanite Religion

The ancestors of the Hebrews had lived in Canaan for three famous generations: the years of Abraham, Isaac, and Jacob. Then a famine drove them to Egypt, where the hero of the fourth generation, Joseph, was in charge. His brothers had sold him into slavery, but his skill in dream interpretation and the favor of God helped him move into a very powerful position. For hundreds of years the people later called Hebrews and even later Jews lived in the Nile Delta. Their God's name was YHWH. It is never spoken aloud in Judaism, but may have been pronounced "Yahweh."

THE IDOLS WE WORSHIP

Canaan
ca 1300 BCE

Wall Street
ca 2000 CE

With the passage of time, they lost their land, their rights, and their freedom. They became enslaved, and it was perhaps 400 years before God would send Moses the Prince of Egypt to confront Pharaoh. Moses had been adopted anonymously by his Hebrew slave mother and kept his true identity a secret. The ten plagues were God's way of telling Pharaoh to "let my people go." The Exodus is their story.

Safe on the other side of the Red Sea with Pharaoh and his army drowned, the Hebrews headed for the Promised Land of Canaan. But God warned them, "when you enter the land YHWH your God is giving you, you must not learn the disgusting practices of those nations.' That's how Moses explains it: we're coming to the Promised Land, but don't pick up their religion!

The Hebrews were a disorganized group of ex-slaves, freed by their God from the polytheistic Pharaoh's slavery and destined for their own country. Unfortunately, there were plenty of people already living there.

Anyway, God continues:

"There must never be found among you anyone who sacrifices his son or daughter in the fire, tells fortunes, reads omens, no soothsayers or sorcerers, no one who casts spells or conjures up spirits, no one practicing the occult, or pretends to speak to the dead. God forbids and detests these things, and is going to drive these people out of the land before you. But you must also be blameless when you stand before God. These nations you are about to dispossess listen to omen-readers and diviners, but God gives you no permission to do these things."

(Deuteronomy 18:10-22)

The Chosen People were going to be tempted in Canaan. So many religions, so many myths, so many gods with their pillars and shrines awaited them. Three months after leaving slavery in Egypt, when Moses was up on Mt. Sinai for a long time speaking with God, the children of Israel made a golden calf to worship. They wanted a god they could lead around by the ring in his nose. They made a baby bull from all the gold jewelry they had been "given" by their owners when they left Egypt. The very first sin after getting the Ten Commandments was breaking Number One (no idols). For the next 1,000 years or more, God kept warning them to be ethical, not superstitious. To worship the one true force in the universe, not the hundreds of fun or scary or exciting or mysterious gods and goddesses who inhabited the towns and mountaintops of Canaan. "I am YHWH your God," says Commandment Number One, "you shall have no other Gods before me."

But it doesn't say, "those other gods do not exist." Many Bible scholars think that at this stage of history (well before 1,000 BCE), the Hebrews were *monolatrous*. You might remember the word from chapter 1. In other words, 'pay no attention to those other gods who will try to get your loyalty. I am the God who got you out of slavery. Put no other Gods ahead of me'.

Among the Canaanite gods were Baal, the local version of the Sky God, and Asherah, his wife, the local version of the Mother Goddess. During a very long drought, the king and queen of Israel, with the memorable names of Ahab and Jezebel, began attending shrines to these and other local gods, and the Jewish prophet Elijah challenged all the local priests to a contest: the World Cup of Religions. Poly versus Mono. It was a match between 850 pagan priests and himself, in which Elijah taunted them and their gods all afternoon: "Sing louder! They must have fallen asleep!" The priests begged the divine Mr. Baal to please send thunder, lightning, and rain from the sky. His opponents failed to ignite the bulls on their altars, and then with one minute left in regulation, and after pouring water all over his sacrifice, Elijah got fire from heaven. He asked, Yahweh delivered. And then a rain cloud appeared on the horizon. The king and queen were humiliated. Instead of a victory lap, and without even waiting for the national anthem, Elijah got the crowd to round up the losers and kill them all. (I Kings 18)

But despite Elijah's triumph over the priests of Baal's Cult, polytheism kept flourishing. In the spring, some of the pagan temples devoted to fertility goddesses offered ceremonies where a farmer would visit a "temple prostitute" for her professional services, which were believed to link the farmer and his fields with the goddess Asherah herself. Money was, of course, required. The book of Leviticus also warns the Chosen People not to offer their children to the bull-god Moloch, whether in some form of slavery or even human sacrifice. It is unknown how many Hebrew children were abused in this way, but the warning makes us think it was a real problem.

Judaism therefore had to compete with many neighboring religions, and not all Jews were as monolatrous as they were supposed to be.

CHAPTER 17

Flood Stories from all over the world

This is perhaps the most terrible thing that could happen to a country: the rain begins to fall and it never stops. The creeks fill up the rivers, and the rivers fill up the lakes and the ocean even starts to rise. All over the Middle East, people tell stories like Noah's. Scholars believe they date from before the Monotheistic Period, Stage four.

A very few people were prepared for the Great Flood. Most were not. A very few animals survived. Most did not. The way they told the story in Babylonia is a little different from the story from Israel: God sends a messenger to Noah in a dream and asks him to bring a few more people on board. In both stories, the flood wipes out the known world.

The Biblical story shows God having already been disappointed by people twice:

1. Eve and Adam ate the forbidden fruit (why?)
2. Cain killed Abel (why?)

But now, God has given up on his invention. 'I wish I hadn't made the world like this. People are so noisy and mean and violent. I thought they were going to be like me. I liked the world better when there were just animals. But maybe if we start over with a really good family—not like Adam and Eve, but people that prove that they can handle some responsibility—well, they can re-populate the earth. Let's see if I can get them to build a lifeboat.'

Some archaeologists working for National Geographic, while diving under the Black Sea in 1999, found something pretty amazing—it had once been a freshwater lake. Thousands of years ago all the villages on the shore of the lake were flooded out. Parts of their houses are still there, under water, far from today's shoreline. When the sea burst in, the Great Flood turned the Black Lake into the Black Sea. Thousands of people were wiped out. Freshwater fish and shellfish died and new ocean species came in. One theory says a tsunami in the Mediterranean caused the breach.

This is a very ancient story. They told it this way in Israel, another way in Babylon, and in still other ways in Iran, Turkey, and the Ukraine. All over the Middle East, they told the story to answer the question, "how could God let this disaster happen?" There are similar stories from North America, too, perhaps based on the inundation of ancient Lake Agassiz.

Your task is to find one or more of these stories, and chart similarities and differences:

- *Were the floods announced beforehand to a good person to help save his family?*
- *Were animals also saved?*
- *Was a boat involved?*
- *Why was the flood sent? Was it a punishment for something?*
- *How long did it last? Did the flood cover the whole world as they knew it?*

PART THREE

The Axial Age

The Tree of World Religions keeps growing. The trunk thickens and the limbs spread. One great branching happened around five or six hundred years BCE. It was an amazing turning point that Karl Jaspers called the "Axial Age." All over the world new, unifying teachers "pivoted" people's consciousness. "What is new about this age, in all...[affected] areas of the world," wrote the German philosopher and psychiatrist, "is that man becomes conscious of Being as a whole, of himself and his limitations." Jaspers further noted: "Measured against the lucid humanity of the Axial Period, a strange veil seems to lie over the most ancient cultures preceding it, as though man had not yet really come to himself."

Supernaturalism focuses on the mysterious, magical, even frightening world of the gods. It's full of miracles behind that strange veil, and not even the greatest human experts can see much on the other side. The Axial Age seems to say: "Pay less attention to the other side of the veil. Let the gods take care of themselves. They gave us a brain. It's time to use it." From Israel to India to China wise thinkers arose in these polytheistic kingdoms with their big cities and specialized workers. Farmers were producing enough surplus to feed all those city-dwellers and support permanent armies. A lot of brainpower went to organizing this much more complex life, and at least some of those brains focused on the biggest questions of human life, but not so much on the afterlife or any kind of spiritual world that might exist "out there."

This section includes three chapters on Buddhism, which is so nontheistic as to be maybe not a religion at all, but surely a great example of Axial Age wisdom.

We'll finish with Socrates, who asked the toughest religious and ethical questions and lost his life for doing it.

CHAPTER 18

The Wise One: Kong Fuzi

In China, the changes of the Axial Age were also turning people from fearful superstition to ethics and morality. Confucianism was founded by an unsuccessful political adviser who lived in the 500s BCE in the eastern province of Shandong. He was known as Kong The Master for his excellent teaching. Like Socrates, he asked questions and loved discussions. He was as much a learner as any of his students ever were. He failed to get high government posts, though he spent many years offering his services. Before his traveling period, which began when he was 50, Kong was a civil servant. He was known for being incorruptible and honest, even blunt sometimes. He was an old-fashioned guy who believed in doing everything the right way, not the easy way.

He died after spending five years in retirement back in his home province, editing Chinese Classics and teaching future leaders. He was saved from being a fanatic by having a great sense of humor, so even when criticizing people, he won their confidence and admiration. His most famous saying, 500 years before Jesus or Rabbi Hillel said the same thing, was the Golden Rule: "Never impose on others what you would not choose for yourself."

He became famous in part because he came along at just the right time. The dynasty of his age, the Chou, was decaying from within. Mass murder, ethnic cleansing, and widespread corruption made people wonder if China could keep from destroying herself. Animals, he reasoned, at least have instincts like self-preservation, but humans have only what they learn. And teach. Tradition worked well in small-scale societies, but China was getting to be

an urbanized nation of states. People were becoming less tribal, and questioned any authority larger than the family. The "mortar" holding the building blocks of society together was flaking away.

Some thinkers at the time — the "Realists" — said, "if you want the peasants to obey, scare them." But unfortunately even if reigns of terror work, the masses hate them. A popular teacher of the day, Mo Ti, on the other hand, proposed a philosophy of love—treat everyone as you would treat your own family, he said, and you won't need rules, tribes, Emperors, or traditions.

Kong didn't agree with either answer, the heavy hand or the soft heart. The Realists could regulate behavior, but not change attitudes. Mo Ti was just too idealistic, and selfish freeloaders would take advantage of all the generosity. Kong researched the China of 500 years before, calling it the Age of Golden Harmony. If the ancestors' ways had been forgotten, he reasoned, it was time to teach them again. The teachers were to work in temples, theatres, homes, and schools. They would use proverbs, history, toys, and stories to instruct people in the old ways.

A student asked, "What would you say of the person who is liked by all his fellow townspeople?" Kong Fuzi replied, "Just being liked isn't enough. The better man is liked by the good and hated by the bad!" He also said, "The well-bred are dignified but not pompous. The ill-bred are pompous, but not dignified." Here are just five basic moral ideas from Master Kong. There are so many more, worthy of research. If you are studying Chinese, find out what the radicals of each character mean.

 Rén — benevolence, kindheartedness, humanity

 Jūn.zi — a man of noble character

 Li — respect for ceremony, proper behavior, etiquette

Dé — virtue, moral character

Wén — accomplishment in the arts of peace, including calligraphy, poetry, and composition

The best society is not individualistic, then, but relational. The web of loyalties, duties, and satisfactions makes each person less important than the quality of the community. People were advised to think less of self and more of the whole. This led to veneration of ancestors, and a religion of the here and now.

Confucianism sees itself as a religion, because it teaches that there are Heavenly and Earthly Realms. The ancestors in heaven must be respected, and sacrifices made to the whole family tree of human ancestors, right on up to the first one, the ultimate ancestor, Shang Ti. A ruler will earn the Mandate of Heaven with noble behavior, and Heaven will not shine for long on unjust rulers. A junzi will always keep the Will Of Heaven in mind; so he or she must be at least a bit religious. But Kong the Master turned the religious emphasis from the Will of Heaven to the Ethics of Earth.

CHAPTER 19

The Ancient Master: Laozi

Daoism started with a man from a western state in China, born a generation before Kong Fuzi. The younger man was very impressed the one time he met the older one. Laozi was a librarian, a scholar like Kong Fuzi, but not as involved in government. The story goes that Laozi was disappointed at people's lack of interest in his teaching, a wisdom based on nature itself. As he rode his water buffalo into retirement in the west, the gatekeeper at the border asked him to stay a bit longer and write down some of his beliefs.

The result was 5000 characters, a collection of poems that you can read in half an hour and re-read for a lifetime. The book, Dao De Jing, is often called "the wisest book ever written." Its title means "The Way and Its Power." Dao is the subject of the book, and of the religion. It's a word with many meanings.

- *The Way of the Universe*, the rhythm of existence, a vast flow of energy within, behind, and beneath all things
- *The Mother of All Things*, giving life to every sort of matter and energy in the universe.
- *The Way of Life*, the path which we ought to follow, sometimes called wu wei, a frictionless, flexible kind of movement, a journey of effortlessness and natural grace.
- *The Truth of Existence*, unchanging, reliable, and good.

Daoism has not just been a philosophy, though. A lot of Chinese medicine, many of the martial arts, and most Chinese religion is based on the Dao. Daoism works with chi, the natural force flow in all living beings, and which is the basis of acupuncture and the prayer/ meditation/ exercise form called Tai Chi. The fortune-telling practice *I Ching* comes from Daoism.

Of the four primal elements (earth, air, water, and fire) Daoism admires water the most—it supports things and carries them along effortlessly on its tide. Poor swimmers flail, but good swimmers float without fighting. Water adapts its shape instantly, yet is strong enough to carve canyons. Daoism enjoys paradoxes: "The journey of 1,000 miles begins with a single step." "The one who knows does not speak. The one who speaks does not know."

Finally, there is the famous Yin / Yang. It expresses the flowing, flexible nature of the Dao. Each side of this force has within it the seed of its opposite. Darth Vader has some goodness in him, and the nicest person in the world harbors some evil thoughts. Even though Yang / Yin seems to be about the dividedness of reality, it symbolizes unity.

- yin/yang
- cool/hot
- matter/spirit
- relaxed/rapid
- tranquil/energetic
- night/day
- female/male
- water/dry land
- moon/sun

Your author published a TED-Ed talk on the meanings of yin and yang: https://youtu.be/ezmR9Attpyc

Here are three poems from the Dao De Jing, as translated by the poet and Chinese scholar Stephen Mitchell. As you read, gather up the metaphors so you can better picture this invisible Dao:

1. The Dao that can be told
is not the eternal Dao.
The name that can be named
is not the eternal Name.
The unnamable is the eternally real.
Naming is the origin
of all particular things.
Free from desire, you realize the mystery.
Caught in desire, you see only the manifestations.
Yet mystery and manifestations
arise from the same source.
This source is called darkness.
Darkness within darkness.
The gateway to all understanding.

8. The supreme good is like water,
which nourishes all things without trying to.
It is content with the low places that people disdain.
Thus it is like the Dao.
In dwelling, live close to the ground.
In thinking, keep to the simple.
In conflict, be fair and generous.
In governing, don't try to control.
In work, do what you enjoy.
In family life, be completely present.
When you are content to be simply yourself
and don't compare or compete, everybody will respect you.

61. When a country obtains great power,
it becomes like the sea:
all streams run downward into it.
The more powerful it grows,
the greater the need for humility.
Humility means trusting the Dao,
thus never needing to be defensive.
A great nation is like a great man:
When he makes a mistake, he realizes it.
Having realized it, he admits it.
Having admitted it, he corrects it.
He considers those who point out his faults
as his most benevolent teachers.
He thinks of his enemy as the shadow that he himself casts.
If a nation is centered in the Dao,
if it nourishes its own people
and doesn't meddle in the affairs of others,
it will be a light to all nations in the world.

CHAPTER 20

The Enlightened One: Buddha

Just as Christianity would someday grow from Judaism because of Jesus, Buddhism grew out of Hinduism because of Siddhartha Gotama. Called "Buddha" by his followers, his title means "awake." He's maybe the perfect example of the Axial Age: moving away from superstition, criticizing the straitjacket of the caste system, and telling people not to think about the gods or afterlife, but instead focus on The Real Life: this one.

The night he was conceived, his mother had a vivid dream of an elephant (symbol of wisdom and eternity) blessing her and even dancing with her. Little Siddhartha was the son of a noble couple in Northern India about 600 years BCE, and was such a remarkable child that a prophet declared he would either be the ruler of all India or the savior of the world. A ruler himself, his father wanted him to follow the path of power, wealth, and fame; and thus he resolved not to do anything to let his son even know that the world needed some kind of "saving." Moments after his birth, which gave his mother no pain, he could speak. He took his first steps and lotus blossoms appeared in his newborn's footprints.

According to legend, the prince was shielded from all suffering, and when he finally went outside the palace walls, he was shocked to see people ill, growing old, and mourning the death of others. He was moved with compassion. He also saw a wandering pilgrim, a Hindu man in the fourth stage of life. Sickness, Old Age, Death, and this Holy Man became known as the Buddha's Four Sights.

He was a good Hindu, but making sacrifices to gods or pilgrimages to shrines did not seem enough to him. He questioned why religion should emphasize rituals to merely soothe the suffering. He was impatient. He knew there must be a prescription to end suffering, and that all people, not just high-caste ones like himself, ought to be capable of the effort. He felt sure that blindly doing your duty (dharma) dictated by your caste was not the best guide to your actions. And do we really have to wait for thousands of lifetimes to escape the curse of suffering? Why could a poor or uneducated person not reach the highest levels, if they worked hard at it?

He gave up the life of a prince. One night, he and his servant Channa took his white horse and left the palace for good. His wife and small son were left behind. Skipping the rest of the householder stage and the retired stage, he went right to becoming a wandering pilgrim. He tried fasting to the point of what we would now call anorexia. He swore off all pleasures, becoming an ascetic (denying all but the bare necessities of life). But even as a perfect wandering pilgrim, neither he nor his fellows were happy. Renunciation alone was not the answer.

Legend has it that he lost consciousness in a river, perhaps delirious with hunger, perhaps in a moment of insight, and a village girl found him. He had just heard a teacher telling his music student not to tighten the string too much, lest it break; but also not to let it go too slack, for it would make no sound. This was, he realized, the story of his life. He had gone from extreme luxury to extreme poverty. Neither extreme brought him happiness. Was the answer somewhere in between? So he accepted the village girl's offer of food and emptied the bowl. Then, seeking a sign that his idea of moderation was true, he asked the river to let the bowl float upstream, against the current. And it did, causing the village girl to take her bowl and run, frightened, back home. He began eating in moderation, and in the course of a seven-day meditation, seated in the Lotus position under a Bodhi tree, he became enlightened.

He had resolved to either die sitting there or to diagnose the source of suffering. He was tempted, as Jesus later would be, by all kinds of attractive and seductive demons which tried to persuade him to give up his quest. The tempter was called Mara, who tried every trick he could think of: dancing girls, food, a frightening serpent, but to no avail. He was determined to find the answer. On the seventh day, it came to him in a flash: Enlightenment.

Now I know why we suffer, he smiled to himself, *and we can do something about it.*

CHAPTER 21

Buddhism

Sitting there, under the Bodhi tree around 600 years BCE, Siddhartha was doing his part to spin India on its Axis. His answer would later be called The Four Noble Truths:

- Life is "dukkha" (out of joint, off-center, painful, broken).
- Dukkha is caused by "tanha," a selfish craving for private fulfillment at the expense of others.
- If you remove that tanha, you will be free of dukkha, and live an enlightened, joyful life, perhaps escaping the wheel of reincarnation.
- Removing tanha is difficult, but possible, if you follow the Noble Eightfold Path.

What's that? Well, it's like eight spokes on a wheel on which you can roll down the path of enlightenment.

TWO SPOKES OF WISDOM

   i. Right View, beginning with the Four Noble Truths
   ii. Right Intentions, focusing on life's best goals

THREE SPOKES OF GOOD BEHAVIOR

   iii. Right Speech, resolving to be always truthful and reflect on our failures to be truthful
   iv. Right Action, following the Five Precepts
       1. Do Not Kill
       2. Do Not Steal
       3. Do Not Lie
       4. Do Not Be Unchaste
       5. Do Not Drink Intoxicants

   v. Right Livelihood (Work) taking only jobs that promote and do not destroy life

THREE SPOKES OF MEDITATION:

vi. Right Effort, moving steadily toward enlightenment without quitting
vii. Right Concentration, practicing meditation like the Buddha so as to reach enlightenment
viii. Right Mindfulness, looking deeply inward at regular times

A new religion was born under that tree, because people immediately recognized that Siddhartha had something worth giving everything up for. He radiated joy, simplicity and wisdom. He lived exactly what he taught. Many chose to become monks or nuns and follow him. To do so, they had to promise nonviolence (which extended to animals, so they were vegetarian), honesty, sexual purity, and swear off all intoxicants. They lived in harmony with their community, and owned little or nothing.

Unlike Hinduism, Buddhism preached that everyone, regardless of their social caste, could escape dukkha by (step-by-step) letting go of tanha. Like Hinduism, Buddhists believed in the cycle of rebirths, but they differed about the end of it. In Hinduism, remember, moksha happens when you spin off the cycle and your small bit of soul joins the Big Everything (Brahman). For Buddhists, leaving the cycle puts you in a place called Nirvana, which is no-place, or no-thing. It could be considered the Big Nothing.

Or look at it like this: everyone lives like a candle flame. When a candle burns down, you light a new one from the old, and the first one dies. There isn't a soul that gets passed on, but your ideas and emotions, like the flame, move to the next life. Reincarnation, the Buddha said, is more like a chain of causes and effects.

Well, what about bad karma? What about being reborn at a lower or higher level based on how good or bad you were at doing your dharma? The Buddha didn't take the caste system very seriously. He agreed that your karma moves from candle to candle, but not that a new candle is higher or lower in status than the old. The problem that holds us back is dukkha, not caste.

If nothing is permanent, and we don't have souls, then enlightenment—not moksha—becomes the goal. Buddhist enlightenment happens in THIS life; and when an Enlightened One dies, their work on earth is done. They become no-thing in a no-place called Nirvana. Hindu moksha ushers you into Brahman, the soul of everything.

However, a person may choose NOT to go on to Nirvana, even though they deserve the reward. They taste the bliss and joy, but decide to go back across the river of life and help others find true happiness. These saints are the great Buddhas and Lamas of Buddhism, the Zen Masters and the Roshis, the teachers and guides who choose to be reincarnated again. Many sects of Buddhism believe that a reincarnated Lama (the most famous one is the Dalai Lama) will have a huge head-start on enlightenment in their next life, and thus can lead many people across the river of life.

Here are some of the biggest sects of Modern Buddhism:

MAHAYANA

Mostly found in northern Asia: China, Tibet, Japan, Korea, and Mongolia. Their sacred language is Sanskrit, but many local languages are widely used. They have many ceremonies and festivals. The goal is to become enlightened with the help of others so as to escape samsara forever and enter Nirvana, BUT many decide to postpone that escape and help others attain it also. Mahayana means the "bigger raft," because of this desire to help others get across the river of life.

THERAVADA

Mostly found in southern Asia: Sri Lanka, Thailand, Burma, Laos, Cambodia. Their sacred language is Pali, and it's important to learn that language. They have fewer ceremonies or festivals. The goal is to become enlightened through individual effort and escape samsara forever. To do this, you need training as a monk for at least some of your life. While you might want to help others reach Nirvana after you do, that goal is not as popular in Theravada. Thus, it is called the smaller raft.

ZEN

A branch of Mahayana Buddhism, zen is the best-known form in the Americas and Europe, as well as its homelands of Japan and China. Zen rejects scriptures, rituals, festivals, and other religious activities in favor of disciplined imitation of the Buddha's meditation, usually under the supervision of a Zen Master. We'll focus more on Zen in the next chapter.

PURE LAND

A branch of Mahayana Buddhism. Now the dominant type of Buddhism in Japan, Pure Land teaches that humans cannot attain Nirvana from this earth. It is necessary to lead a good life and go to the Pure Land, where all see the truth. From that heavenly world, Nirvana can be reached.

TIBETAN

Neither Mahayana or Theravada. When Buddhism came to Tibet, it absorbed some beliefs about reincarnation that led to the modern system of reincarnating lamas. Tenzin Gyatso, the Dalai Lama, for example, is known as the 14th incarnation (since 1357). They also believe in many gods, have elaborate ceremonies, and much art devoted to understanding and pleasing the gods.

The Vietnamese monk Thich Nhat Hanh

CHAPTER 22

Zen Buddhism

Buddhism is all about reducing dukkha by giving up tanha. Zen Buddhism is a branch that especially loves to shake up people who think too much. That's why this chapter is so short: Zen is not about a lot of words. Getting enlightened is not like a math problem or a science experiment. It's like a piece of music or a good joke.

The word "zen" is the Japanese pronunciation of the original Middle Chinese word "chán." Zen is the name for the serene mind which meditators achieve and which nourishes their daily life.

In class, we will play with some Zen puzzles, called koans, which might help you understand the Buddhist approach to salvation: simple, disciplined, practical, and virtuous.

- Here's a funny video about a martial arts master studying zen, disturbed by a fly: https://www.youtube.com/watch?v=HsoswhGCkeY
- Here's another one, in which the great Zen teacher Alan Watts comments on who we are talking about when we call ourselves "I." http://youtu.be/OAVM_Xk_o9E
- And here is a whole facebook page full of cartoons about zen. Maybe you can get a bit closer to enlightenment with them: https://www.facebook.com/ZenCartoons

Zen Master Wendy Egyoku Nakao, head of the Los Angeles Zen Center

CHAPTER 23

The Questioner: Socrates

The most dangerous thing about Socrates? He knows that he *doesn't know very much*. So writes Jostein Gaarder in *Sophie's World*. An oracle in Athens pronounced Socrates the wisest man in the city, but rather than answering the many questions of strangers and friends in the marketplace, all Socrates would do was ask more questions. You would think he was stupid at first. Then you might think he was just pretending to be stupid. But, Socrates explained, he learned it from his mother, a midwife. Just as midwives help women give birth, just so should a good teacher help bring out the knowledge students already have inside. The word "educate" means "to draw out." Socrates spent his days asking people questions and then getting into conversations about the most important things in life.

One day, Socrates was on his way to court, accused of teaching the youth of Athens religious falsehoods and lack of respect for the gods. He met a religious expert named Euthyphro, who was coming to file charges against his own father, accused of manslaughter. It seems that his father had had one of his workers bound, gagged, and thrown in a ditch for killing one of the family slaves. Euthyphro's father sent a message to the priests, asking how he should punish the murderer. The answer was so long in coming that the worker in the ditch died from exposure to the wind, rain, and cold. So now the father was a murderer! But Socrates was very surprised: shouldn't Euthyphro be more loyal to his father? Shouldn't he hold back and let the relatives of the dead person file charges, as the law required?

'Since I am here to defend myself against the charge that I have disrespected the gods, maybe I can learn something from you about the gods and goodness,' Socrates begins. 'Is everything the gods command good?' He reminds Euthyphro of the god Cronos castrating his own father, Uranus, just to get the conversation going.

'It would seem that the gods are cruel and inconsistent. So how can we rely on their commands?' Socrates wanted to know what "morally good" means. Maybe Euthyphro could give him a good definition. Euthyphro tried at least three times, but fails.

60

Euthyphro: Morally good? It's like what I am doing now: bringing charges against my father for doing the wrong thing, even though I don't want my father to get in trouble.

Socrates: That's an example, not a definition.

Euthyphro: Well, then: moral goodness is doing that which pleases the gods.

Socrates: Good answer. After all, who knows better than the gods?

Euthyphro: Right!

Socrates: But what if one god likes something and another does not? Which one is right? The gods often seem pretty inconsistent to me.

Euthyphro: Shhhhhh! You shouldn't talk like that. That's what got you into trouble, Socrates. But I suppose something is good only if all the gods approve. If they all disapprove, then the thing is surely wrong.

Socrates: OK, but is it good because the gods approve or do they approve because it is good?

Euthyphro: The second, I suppose. The gods approve of good things.

Socrates: They could not approve of bad things? Or command us to do a bad thing?

Euthyphro: Well, yes, they could. They are the gods. They do what they wish.

Socrates: Well, it sounds like goodness isn't up to the gods, then. It's bigger than the gods! The gods must obey it.

In other words, if things are good or bad because the gods command them, and if the will of the gods must always be obeyed, then God could have told Moses, "Thou Shalt Commit Murder," and murder would have been, from that day onward, good. But reason tells us God never would have commanded that. A good god is not arbitrary.

Socrates was saying that goodness does not depend on religion, and reason is a more trustworthy guide than blind faith. Here's a cartoon about Euthyphro and Socrates from the anti-religion website Jesusandmo.com. It pretty much sums up the big question of the Axial Age.

PART FOUR

Three Abrahamic Monotheisms

Abraham probably lived a thousand years before Socrates, but his story in Genesis was the product of the Axial Age. The Jewish family tree goes back to his son Isaac and wife, Sarah. The Arabic and later Muslim line goes back to his son Ishmael whose mother was Hagar.

Jews regard Abraham as the first patriarch, whose Covenant or solemn agreement with future generations would be sealed by circumcision and animal sacrifices. If those generations worshipped this God alone, they would become as numerous as the stars and take ownership of a land between Egypt and the Euphrates River.

Christians see Abraham as the first real monotheistic believer. He did not live to see his promises fulfilled, but who passed on his faith to Isaac and Rebekah, who in turn would extend what was becoming a Divine Blessing to their son Jacob, and his sons, who would become the twelve tribes of Israel. Jesus the Messiah would be part of the tribe of the youngest, Benjamin.

Muslims revere him as a prophet, like Adam, Moses, Jesus, and finally Muhammad. In Islam, Abraham and Ishmael rebuilt the House (known as the *kaaba*) of the One God, Allah. Their faith was proven by the famous near-sacrifice, but with a twist: in Islam, the son is thought to have been Ishmael.

We'll study them in chronological order.

Other religions, including the Baha'i, Druze, Yazidis, Samaritans, and Rastafarians, also trace their origins to Abraham.

CHAPTER 24

The Faithful One: Abraham

There was no "Judaism" at first. It wasn't a belief, but a relationship between a couple and their God. After Abraham heard God call him, he and his wife Sarah became monolatrous. The Bible only hints at Abraham's early life, but oral tradition describes his father serving the polytheistic Babylonian king Nimrod with gusto, praying to idols and making sacrifices at every temple in town.

Abraham and Sarah believed instead the singular voice that beckoned them west to a Promised Land, the voice that promised them descendants as numerous as the stars in the night sky. Their adventures are colorful, including two narrow escapes when they pretended to be brother and sister in order to avoid Abraham being killed and Sarah captured. When they finally had a son, it was by her slave, Hagar. They adopted the boy, Ishmael, but Sarah still wanted a biological son, and God finally helped her conceive. This son was Isaac.

When the boys were older, God asked Abraham if he would sacrifice his son. The Bible describes Abraham taking Isaac to the Holy Mountain and being ready, with knife on hand, to carry out this primitive and awful act of loyalty. But then God sent an angel to tell Abraham to stop.

Modern rabbis argue about this test. Most say that Abraham passed because he proved his willingness to obey his God. It was a test of his faith in God. Other rabbis say no! He was willing to do evil just because God told him to. He therefore *failed* the test. God had given Abraham the test by speaking to him directly, but stopped it just in time by sending his angel, not to congratulate him, but to halt the killing. According to this interpretation, God learned that Abraham still had the primitive mind of fearful submission.

This is the Axial Age in a single, brilliant moment: was it a good act because God commanded it, or can God command only good acts?

Abraham's near-sacrifice of his son

The Qur'an tells the story differently: Abraham dreamed that he was slaughtering his son. He told him the dream the next morning, and the son said that, if this dream came from God, he was willing. God saw this willingness, and praised both of them. One cannot tell from the story whether God sent the dream or it was some awful nightmare, but the Qur'an takes the Axial view: no human sacrifice. Most Muslim writers say that the son in the story was Ishmael, the ancestor of the Arab people. Jews and Christians believe it was Isaac.

Isaac and his wife Rebekah had twin sons, Jacob and Esau, whose story is fascinating and complicated. Jacob carried the blessing forward with the help of his mom, and had twelve sons. They became the heads of the twelve tribes of Israel. The most famous son, Joseph, was sold by his jealous brothers into slavery in Egypt, and turned out to be even wiser about dreams than his great-grandfather Abraham. He knew that God spoke to him in dreams, and meant him to lead his family and eventually the whole country of Egypt. His skill with dream interpretation got him out of prison and into the office of the Pharaoh. Joseph then convinced him to buy up huge surpluses of grain because famine was coming. And indeed it did. The result was a very wealthy Pharaoh thanking the Israelites (they were still not Jews yet) by giving them land.

But centuries went by and these Hebrew foreigners grew poor, lost their land, and eventually were enslaved by the Egyptians. When they remembered God at all, they knew him as "The God of Our Fathers," referring to Abraham, Isaac, and Jacob. Most of the gods the Hebrew slaves knew were from Egyptian polytheism: arbitrary, cruel, and capable of anything. The glimpse Abraham had gotten of a higher god was forgotten.

CHAPTER 25

Judaism: God and the Prophets

The Bible contains the stories of 56 prophets. Here are just three: Moses the liberator, Amos the angry one, and Hosea the sad one.

MOSES THE LIBERATOR

Soon after Moses was born, his Hebrew mother, a slave, put him in a little basket-boat floating in the Nile. Pharaoh had ordered all Hebrew slave-baby boys killed. She chose a place to launch the "ark" where Pharaoh's daughter would be sure to find him and take pity on him. The boy was raised in Pharaoh's household, his identity a secret, perhaps even to himself. When Moses grew up and killed a slave-driver who was whipping a Hebrew, he fled and began a new life among the nomad Midians in the desert.

But the God of the Hebrews had plans to establish himself, "YHWH," as the greatest of the gods. His name is a riddle: it could mean "I Am," or "I Am Who I Am," or even "I'll be who I'll be." It's not a name at all, nor is the divine title "Lord."

Speaking to Moses from a mysterious flaming bush which did not burn up, The Lord told Moses to go liberate the Hebrews from slavery. He gave Moses many assurances, and after the famous ten plagues, they were allowed to leave Egypt. Pharaoh, worshipped as a god himself, then changed his mind, and chased the slaves to the Red Sea. The Lord drowned him and all his army there. "There is no god like you,

God speaks to Moses from the Burning Bush

O Lord," declared the freed Hebrews and yet within a short time, they would make an idol of a god for themselves from looted Egyptian gold: the Golden Calf.

It would be quite a struggle for the prophets of The Lord to get people to stop being polytheistic. At first, they were monolatrous (there are other gods, but only one god for us). The Ten Commandments began with: "I am the Lord your God. You shall have no other gods before me." In other words, he's number one. The others have to stand in line behind Him.

In Moses' early career, his job was to announce the great deeds of the mighty Lord. But late in his life, the emphasis changed toward teaching, the mitzvot or commandments to live a holy and virtuous life. This change is what the Axial Age was about, from east to west. The human mind was turning, seemingly on a huge mental axis, from supernatural mystery to ethics. But, in their palaces, kings clung to polytheism. So did peasants in their villages.

AMOS THE ANGRY ONE

Amos was a farmer who God called to move to the city. He soon got into trouble, by accusing the king of plotting to silence him. But Amos didn't just criticize the king. Rich men were kicking peasants off the land, and those who remained were forced to plant cash crops like grapes for wine or olives for oil. Cash crops are okay when prices are good, because the cash is enough to buy food for your family; but good years were few. Amos described a Day of Reckoning. It was not going to be a good day. The lucky few had it good, but only because they built their wealth, power, fame, and holiness on the backs of widows, orphans, and slaves. They ignored the homeless.

Amos sarcastically quotes God, sitting up in heaven, fed up with all the religious noise:

Homeless man sitting by ATM begging with a Starbucks cup

I despise your festivals! I get no pleasure from your religious assemblies!
Even if you make a burnt offering, I will not be satisfied.
I will not look with favor on your peace offerings of fattened calves.
Take away from me your noisy songs.
I don't want to hear the sound of your stringed instruments.
Instead let justice roll down like waters
And righteousness like a mighty stream. (Amos 5)

HOSEA THE SAD ONE

Hundreds of years later, God, a man named Hosea was convinced he knew how God felt. "Why don't you love me anymore?" Neighboring tribes had so many colorful gods and shrines to choose from. Temptation got the better of God's Chosen People. God even inspired Hosea to marry a notoriously promiscuous woman. She didn't even love him. A good story grabbed people's attention, and so when the Man of God married a woman of ill repute, a crowd gathered to find out why.

God told me to do this so I could tell you how he feels when you are unfaithful. He tries to love you, but you are promiscuous and go after other gods. He got a good laugh. His new wife kept sleeping around, and they laughed even more. But when he named their kids "God won't have pity" and "No child of mine," the children of Israel got the message: maybe they aren't going to be the Chosen People forever.

Shortly after this, the Assyrian army conquered Israel, and thousands, mostly the wealthy and well-educated, were taken away as prisoners of war. In this painting by the German-born Jewish artist Eugen Spiro, Hosea's wife heads out the door to one of her boyfriends, while the prophet writes about the jilted God who patiently waits for his beloved to come home.

During the Axial Age (800-400 BCE), what we now know as Judaism came to life: people were expected to change the world, not make sacrifices to God in the hopes he would do it for them. God became less the stage-manager of the human drama and more the oft-neglected hero. In Richard Elliott Friedman's *The Disappearance of God*, he describes what happens to the main character in the Bible. At first, God dominates the stage, but gradually human beings take over. In one of the last books written, the story of Esther, God does not appear at all. Friedman notes that Nietzsche (1844-1900), by declaring "the death of God," just takes the plot forward.

In Elie Wiesel's novel, Night, about the death camps of World War II, he mourns silence of God. At one point, while the inmates are made to witness a hanging, a man asks, "Where is God?" And inside himself, the narrator knows the answer: "He is there: hanging on the gallows." Later, a character named Moshe (Moses) is asked by young Eliezer (the voice of the narrator):

> "Why did you pray? A strange question. Why did I live? Why did I breathe?"
>
> After that day I saw {Moshe} often. He explained to me with great insistence that every question possessed a power that did not lie in the answer. "Man raises himself toward God by the questions he asks Him," he was fond of repeating. "That is the true dialogue.
>
> Man questions God and God answers. But we don't understand His answers. We can't understand them. Because they come from the depths of the soul, and they stay there until death. You will find the true answers, Eliezer, only within yourself!"
>
> "And why do you pray, Moshe?" I asked him.
>
> "I pray to the God within me that He will give me the strength to ask Him the right questions."

For Jews, God is not just "out there" or "up there." God is within each person, and religion is all about questioning what that means.

CHAPTER 26

Judaism: Meaningfulness

THE MEANING OF GOD

This is one of the smallest religions we will study, in terms of the number of members, but Judaism is one of the three or four most influential religions. It gave birth to Christianity, helped form Islam, and shaped many later religions. Its scriptures and scholars molded much of Western Civilization.

To understand Judaism you have to understand God. The Supreme Being, unlike human beings, does not create itself. Further, that being is beyond our control. In other words, God is "Other." But if God is not human, neither is He a Thing, a Force, or a Principle. God, the Torah and the Prophets declare over and over, is not a person, but God IS personal, mysterious, and alive.

Moses discovered the oneness of God. The neighboring tribes assigned a god to each major power of nature, but Adonai, creator of heavens and earth, has a single supreme will and is Lord of all being. Unlike Greek gods, God was moral and cared—passionately—about human beings. Amos said God was angry with the Jews for ignoring him. Hosea said God was still broken-hearted about it.

THE MEANING OF HUMANITY

In the first chapter of Bereshit (a Hebrew word. The word "Genesis" is Greek), God announces that each day's creation was "very good." Jews look positively on the material world. It isn't corrupt, or inferior, or sinful, but good. Further, the world is there for us to use constructively. Human beings may be made from the dust of the earth, but we have the breath of God in our nostrils, too. We're kind of complicated.

Huston Smith sums up human nature: We are weak by animal standards, but intelligent. We miss the target a lot of the time, but we're still God's beloved children. We can produce great works of artistic beauty and awful destruction. We are free creatures, but also have big responsibilities. We run from God but also seek Him. Unlike Christianity with its doctrine of Original Sin, Jewish teaching holds that humans are born free of sin, but with two gravitational forces tugging inside us: the pull toward doing good and the pull toward doing wrong. To sin (*cheyt*) is to "miss the mark," so a lifetime of practice gradually improves one's aim. As we will see, Islam and Christianity have similar but different explanations of human failure.

Ein Sof, the infinity of God

70

All over the ancient world, Jewish morality was admired, because their God set a very high standard. In the Torah, there are 613 commandments, but four are worth a special look. Each concerns a danger zone in human life:

- • Force—bicker all you want, but do not take the life of anyone in your tribe, because blood feuds never end: **Thou Shall Not Commit Murder.**
- • Wealth—go ahead and make money, compete, be clever, but you can't take things from others: **Thou Shall Not Steal.**
- • Sex—flirt if you want, even be promiscuous, although we frown on that, but once someone marries, they are off-limits: **Thou Shall Not Commit Adultery.**
- • Speech—you ought to speak honestly, but if you tell little white lies, or weasel around a bit, or gossip, well, okay. But once you end up in front of the judge, under oath, no more funny business: **Thou Shall Not Bear False Witness.**

To keep this morality alive, God did not just send the commandments. He also sent prophets who spoke on behalf of God and criticized both individual and social immorality. Whether it was Nathan publicly accusing the greatest king of Israel of murder and adultery or Hosea accusing the fashionable and wealthy of going after other gods like a drunken man goes after whores, the prophets were tough guys. Elijah mocked Queen Jezebel's religion, and Amos told people that God could care less about religious ceremonies if they ignored the poor. God was not just the God of *shalom* (peace) but also *zedekah* (justice).

MEANING IN HISTORY

Huston Smith also credits Jews for being among the first to note that context is everything, and that collective social action can change the world. God wants us to learn from history, not to throw up our hands in despair, believing ourselves to be helpless pawns in a cosmic chess game. Further, although history repeats itself (it rhymes, Mark Twain said), history is also full of unique people and unrepeatable choices. Jacob wrestled with God. Moses said yes to the voice from the burning bush. Ruth and Naomi stuck together, despite tribal differences. David, when confronted with his adultery, confessed immediately to taking advantage of Bathsheba.

Early in God's relationship with the descendants of Abraham, the idea of the Jews being "chosen" came along. At first, this meant that God would guarantee them land and children in return for faithful monotheism. Many generations later, in slavery, the promise was renewed: "I have heard your cries, and I will set you free." By the time of David's son Solomon (a bit later than 1000 BCE) the joint kingdoms of Judah and Israel were about as big as they would ever be.

As Assyria and Babylonia began the downfall of Israel in the 700s BCE, God's time of intervening in Jewish history seemed to be ending. Like the parent of a teenager who sees that her daughter has to deal with the results of her own mess-ups, God pulled back and gave up shielding his chosen ones. Prophets explained that God expected them to be much more faithful or suffer the consequences. The children of Israel were no longer to be treated like children. This experiment on God's part seemed harsh, but necessary. God even got credit for helping the Persians and Hasmoneans conquer the Promised Land. And even the Romans.

The Romans crucified 10,000 Jewish men. Jesus would be the most famous one. Empires had chipped away by force at the borders until the Promised Land simply ceased to be a Jewish place at all. The Romans would tear the Temple in Jerusalem apart, leaving only a bit of the massive foundation now known as the Western (or "wailing") Wall. It appeared that the Nation of Israel had been "chosen" only for bad luck.

But that catastrophe was not the end. Rabbinic Judaism developed into a flourishing culture based on study and observance of the law without any more Temple rituals. Collections of the rabbis' wisdom like the Talmud and Midrashim carried the ancient wisdom forward enabling people to retain a sense of sacredness. If there was no Temple for God to dwell in, then it was time to make other holy places. And times.

Jews declared the modern State of Israel in 1948, after the European Holocaust and mass expulsions of Jews from many Middle Eastern countries. Millions of Jews immigrated to the tiny but very strategic country, renewing the ancient scriptural Promise of the Land. Israeli Jews range from atheistic secularists to extremely observant Orthodox. But almost half the population is not Jewish, and these Palestinians (mostly Muslim and Christian) have a very different perspective on the land.

MEANING IN EVERYDAY LIFE

Even if God sent no more Moseses or Davids, and stopped smiting and parting the sea, there was still the Torah, the Book of the Law. No matter where Jews scattered all over the world, they brought the Sabbath, the Passover, the kosher diet, the Hebrew prayers, and the precious scrolls of God's word. They studied, debated, and took on, family by family, community by community, the task of living a holy life. Holiness is not the same thing as perfection. It means something more like seeing the point of everything and every action. A holy person doesn't just say a lot of prayers, according to the rabbis. A holy person lives life as a prayer. Their deeds are worth more than many words.

Perhaps, the later prophets taught, if every Jew would just lead a holy life for one whole day, God would send moshiach (The Messiah). Whether it would be a person, an angelic being, or an age of justice and peace is still anyone's guess. Possible messiahs have come and gone, but none has ushered in God's rule on earth, as far as the Jews are concerned. The first Christians believed that Jesus of Nazareth was the messiah. A group of Jews in Brooklyn in the 1990s hoped that their rabbi, Menachem Schneerson, was.

Some of the things Jews wear to remind them of God are: prayer shawls with fringes (tzitzit), a skullcap (kippah or yarmulke), and prayer lanyards (tefillin) around their arms and foreheads. The most religious or Orthodox men wear untrimmed beards and long, curling side-locks and women wear wigs and headscarves to cover their own hair.

Keeping kosher is a traditional way of shopping, cooking, and eating, by which food is symbolically holy or not. Meat which is butchered with care and respect for the animal is permitted, but never pork. Nor shellfish, or birds of prey, bats, and a few others. One does not mix meat and dairy, so no cheeseburgers or pepperoni pizza. The original commandment about that said not to "boil the meat of a goat in its' mother's milk," which might have been a superstitious practice by non-Jews.

Many Jews touch a tiny scroll containing a verse of the Torah in a container (mezuzah) placed on their doorpost to remind them of their relationship to God every time they go out or come into their homes.

Finally, three daily acts are essential:

1. **prayer** (three times a day is traditional),
2. **Torah study** (preferably with others, and done with both reverence and curiosity), and
3. **acts of charity and kindness.**

Just as some actions are holier than others, so are some days. In the course of a year, observant Jews hear and study the whole Torah, Sabbath by Sabbath. They celebrate many other holidays, many based on God's deliverance of the Jewish People from their foes. Here is a partial list.

- **The Sabbath** stands as the most important holy day, a weekly day of rest in imitation of God who rested on the seventh day of Creation
- **Rosh Hashanah,** the solemn observance of the new year, beginning with the story of Abraham's binding of Isaac
- **Yom Kippur,** the day of atonement, including fasting and asking others' and God's forgiveness
- **Hanukkah,** the festival of lights, commemorating the recapture of the Temple from the Seleucid Empire
- **Purim,** the festival recalling the near-genocide of the Jews at the hands of Persians, in which the secretly-Jewish Queen Esther plays a heroic role
- **Passover,** the eight-day fast of unleavened bread, commemorating the story of the Exodus of Hebrew slaves led by from Pharaoh's Egypt
- **Shavuot,** a springtime festival especially dedicated to the Ten Commandments and is often the date of confirmation ceremonies

The goal of Jewish life is "Tikkun Olam," repairing and healing the world. Tikkun Olam combines the daily holiness of the first rabbis and the deep sense of social responsibility first spoken through the prophets.

From Israelite to Hebrew to Jew, and through the perils of slavery, dispersion, and numerous ethnic cleansings, the Jewish people have endured and thrived, serving as a source of many later religions, especially Christianity and Islam, the other two "Abrahamic" Religions.

CHAPTER 27

Christianity: Jesus

The second of the three global missionary religions began with Jesus of Nazareth. He was no wealthy prince like Siddhartha. He wasn't of priestly lineage, as Hindus would have expected. He was of the House of David, which was one criterion for recognition as Jewish Messiah, but only in the line of his adopted father, Joseph. He wasn't a brilliant statesman, like Muhammad, nor a writer of poetry, like Laozi. He was called a *tekton*, a carpenter or other manual worker.

He was born in the Roman province of Palestine in 4 BCE. He grew up in Nazareth. At about age 30, he was baptized by the prophet John the Baptist, who was proclaiming God's imminent arrival to judge the human race. Jesus had a career of no more than three years as a healer and teacher. He attracted the attention of the Roman authorities and their Jewish collaborators, and was executed by crucifixion. Shortly after his death, stories arose claiming his bodily resurrection, and his fame spread, thanks to his disciples, relatives, and a Hellenized Jew named Saul / Paul.

As to what historians can attest to, that's about it. Everything else we believe—or disbelieve—about Jesus comes from the Gospels and the Epistles. Here are some of the essential beliefs Christians have about Jesus (thanks to the scholar Marcus Borg for this compact summary):

SPIRIT PERSON

He was a man who was in close and regular contact with the invisible (but real) spiritual world. His "spiritual eye" was opened at his baptism, when he saw

God descending on him like a dove, and a voice declaring that he was God's son. He was able to use this spiritual power for many things, apparently, but never magic tricks. He healed people, cast out demons from the afflicted (we would probably now call these schizophrenic or psychotic people), and even calmed storms. Spirit People were rare and prized in the ancient world, but Jesus was not unique.

SOCIAL PROPHET

He offered an alternative "kingdom": a great and inclusive family of God, distinguished by forgiveness and unconditional love. Other Jewish alternatives were:

1. *The Sadducees*, wealthy collaborators with the Romans who came from the élite classes, and did not believe in an afterlife. Unlike them, Jesus associated with the poor, and promoted change.

2. *The Essenes*, world-hating commune-dwellers who were waiting for God to rescue them from the corruption of the flesh. Unlike them, Jesus stayed involved in the world.

3. *The Zealots*, who taught that the only good Roman was a dead Roman. Their friends called them "freedom fighters," and their enemies called them "terrorists." They committed mass suicide atop the mountain fortress of Masada rather than accept capture by the Romans in 135 AD. Unlike the Zealots, Jesus remained non-violent.

4. *The Pharisees*, a very religious group of mostly peasants and poor people devoted to studying scripture and keeping all 613 commandments scrupulously. They hoped to be so pure that God would reward them with the messiah. You could call them "puritans." They taught that following the Holiness Code would allow the Jewish people to become the vanguard of God's takeover of the world. Jesus was a lot like the Pharisees, but stressed God's compassion, while the Pharisees stressed

God's holiness. His arguments with the Pharisees got him in the most trouble. Jesus criticized the Pharisees for labeling people too strictly: clean/unclean, saint/sinner, us/them.

Jesus caught the attention of the Romans, who did not want to hear about equality, or being part of a Kingdom greater than Rome. Jesus became a statistic, one of 10,000 Jews put to death on crosses all over the Empire.

WISDOM TEACHER

Jesus spoke with very unconventional wisdom: Instead of fighting back, shame your enemy by turning the other cheek. Instead of only loving your friends, love your enemies. Instead of respectable people entering heaven first, outcasts and reformed sinners would. Instead of being cautious and calculating, he said, be as simple as children, birds, or flowers. Instead of admiring the wealthy and fabulous, God loves the poor and unlovely. And why should we turn things upside-down like this? To discover God's love, so much more lavish than what we humans call "love."

His upside-down wisdom, extreme humility, love, and embrace of enemies makes Christianity different from many other world religions. This has frequently been forgotten by Christians in positions of power and influence. Even though he was a very confident man who spoke with authority, he was also very humble. His ego was so transparent that people began to say that if God could take on human form, this is what God would look like.

MOVEMENT FOUNDER

His death by crucifixion was followed by his being raised, something most Jews believed would happen only at the end of time. Jesus reappeared in bodily form, but his nature seemed to have changed. People began seeing him in unexpected places. His body seemed real, but then he would disappear. The wounds from his execution were there, but he walked, ate, and spoke with no apparent pain.

Jesus remained Jewish, and never left the country, but his once-demoralized followers did. They suddenly became eloquent and bold. They described receiving the power of the Holy Spirit as if candle flames descended upon them. "The Way" grew in numbers exponentially, and spread quickly throughout the Empire, especially among the less-than-elite. People began carving fish symbols on walls as directional arrows to the location of their Sabbath meals, although conflicts in synagogues would lead within a couple of generations to a split—regular

Jews would worship on Saturday, and the followers of Jesus on Sunday. The word "fish" in Greek (ichthus) was a kind of acronym, for "Jesus Christ, Son of God, Savior."

What probably made Christianity spread the fastest was not just the stories by and about the resurrected rabbi. It was the men and women disciples themselves. They held all their possessions in common. They were absolutely non-violent, even when persecuted. They ignored all kinds of social discrimination (Roman/Barbarian, Jew/Greek, male/female, slave/free). They were joyful. They seemed unafraid of death. They weren't at all self-centered. They seemed unburdened by guilt.

As C. S. Lewis put it, they were In Love.

Far in the future, the light of that Love would dim as it became a separate and highly-organized religion. The Creeds, The Trinity (God's three-dimensional nature of Father, Son, and Holy Spirit), the Church, the Heresies and Schisms, all these lay in the future.

For three hundred years, however, Christianity was a vibrant, experimental, and often underground spiritual movement which took Jewish ethics and Greek mystical spirituality and exported them to the world.

CHAPTER 28

Christianity: Paul

Most of the best ideas in this chapter come from A.N. Wilson's Paul: The Mind of the Apostle

St. Paul should get most of the credit for turning the Jesus movement into a world religion. Born Saul in Asia Minor, he was a Jew living in a mostly-Greek city, Tarsus, in the Roman Empire. As such, he was far more multicultural and well travelled than the Jesus he started out persecuting. Saul travelled to Jerusalem as a young man to study religion, and got a job as one of the Temple guards, whose job it was to keep order in and around the religious center of the city. If they couldn't keep the peace, Rome threatened, Caesar's troops would be happy to occupy the Temple or even tear it down. In 70 A.D., they did it.

Saul heard plenty about the rabbi Jesus who stirred up trouble at Passover and got crucified for it. He heard the stories, and they made him furious:

1. The idea of resurrection was fine, but it was supposed to happen in the afterlife, not this world.
2. The idea of God having a son who comes to earth sounds like Herakles or some Greek myth, not the superior God of Abraham, Isaac, and Jacob.
3. The idea that God would allow the Messiah to be humiliated by Roman crucifixion was ridiculous.

But, on his way to arrest some followers of The Way in Damascus, he had a powerful direct experience in which the Risen Jesus asked him, 'why are you persecuting me?', and striking him blind for three days. Convinced that he was being given a chance to turn his life around, the former persecutor became the most energetic of all disciples, carrying the Gospel all over the Mediterranean world.

Saul blinded on the road to Damascus

Paul's version of Christianity added several important explanations that helped it spread:

- Jesus' bloodshed was a blessing, not a curse: because he had not shirked from his undeserved punishment, Jesus showed how much God loves human beings. Paul was haunted by the cross and ashamed of his role in persecuting Jesus: 'this man died because of our sins.'

- Jesus' resurrection was true, after all: Paul met the Risen Christ, not the living rabbi / carpenter from Nazareth.

- Jesus proved that the grace of God is stronger than the power even of the greatest empire in history, Rome. God's seeming weakness and foolishness turned out to be more powerful than Roman oppression.

- Jesus showed the limitations of Jewish law: follow it in spirit, not legalistically.

Paul travelled by Roman roads, focused on the biggest cities, started up churches, and moved on. He let the city churches spread the word to smaller towns and villages nearby. At first, he went straight to the synagogues, but then spent more and more time with non-Jews, the so-called "God Fearers" who were open to non-ethnic ways of following God. The God Fearers were interested in becoming "Jew-ish" without becoming Jews (which would require circumcision, kosher eating, clothing, rules about modesty, and rules against marrying non-Jews).

He was troubled by the contradiction of his own Judaism: the whole world comes to respect the Torah, but are shut out. By opening his churches to non-Jews, Paul proclaimed the Eternal, Universal Christ.

Paul also felt keenly how he hadn't come to know Christ by his own efforts, but instead by the gift of that event on the Damascus Road. As a result, his writings emphasized our human inability to earn or deserve God's love. We can hardly improve ourselves, he said, much less perfect ourselves. In fact, over and over, we do what we don't want to do. We need God's love, even if we can never pay it back.

The Emperor Claudius expelled all Jews from Rome itself in about the year 51 CE, because of their continuing disturbances at the instigation of their leader 'Chrestus.' He misspelled 'Christ' and didn't seem to know that he was dead: how could he be causing trouble? The élites in Rome had learned to fear the Jews. For this unusual time in their history, Jews were making converts. We now think that only Christianity has missionaries, but Judaism did so, too, with a lot of success. Why?

For one thing, they had high moral standards. Public religion in Rome was immature, greedy, and full of gluttony and sexual misconduct. The God-Fearers were seen as grown-ups among adolescent fools. The incest, bigamy, murder, and easy divorces of the Roman upper class led to general disgust with their polytheism. It was obvious that the Jews had a superior way of life.

But for another thing, in the eyes of the gentiles (non-Jews) of the day, what really made Judaism seem special is that it had superior magic powers. Alexander the Great had worshipped YHWH, the four-letter name of God on the headdress of the High Priest in Jerusalem. Everyone knew that. The Jews had a God who was so powerful that *you were not even allowed to say His Name.* Magicians all over the empire bought and treasured copies of the Hebrew Scriptures. The Jewish God had put planets in their orbits! Jesus himself was best known, not for his Sermon on the Mount or his Golden Rule, but as the man who stopped a storm, withered a fig-tree, and commanded evil spirits.

In Europe, Paul made his first convert: Lydia, a wealthy textile dyer who specialized in purple, the most expensive color. Her large house became home base for the church in her town. Women joined Christianity as leaders as well as followers, and Paul welcomed their friendship.

Later on, in Athens, Paul explained that his God was not anything new: he showed them the statue of "An Unknown God," and identified him: The One True God, maker of all things who does not need human beings to do anything for him. To the contrary: God has done much for human beings.

After four journeys around Greece, Italy, Asia Minor, Arabia, and Israel, Paul got arrested by the Temple Guards in Jerusalem. Ironic, of course: he had once been one of them. He insisted on a trial in front of Caesar, because he was a Roman citizen. That was unusual for a Jew in those days, and he was smuggled down to a prison ship in Caesarea during the night, for fear of assassins.

A fourteen-day storm ensued, finally throwing his ship on the shore of Malta, where a viper bit him. When he didn't get sick, the guards decided that he was a god. They delivered him to Rome where he lived under house arrest, awaiting trial. He received guests from the new church there, and letters from churches throughout the Empire. He wrote letters of advice, some of which have been preserved in the New Testament as Epistles. Paul never intended for centuries of people to read his mail, but his ideas are absolutely essential to Christianity. He was probably executed in Rome, 30 years or so after his Lord.

Chapter 29

Christianity: Creeds and Heresies

By the time Paul died, the map of Christianity would have been a bunch of dots on cities around the Mediterranean, most densely-concentrated in the Holy Land. Here is a great animated map of what happened next: https://youtu.be/sPudO9NjdBE

Nero blamed a large fire in Rome on Christians, and the persecutions began. Many churches met underground to avoid harassment. They chose bishops, priests, and deacons to lead the growing religion with its Greek New Testament and Jewish God. For a while, the greatest Christians were martyrs who preferred death rather than renouncing loyalty to their Lord. Jesus had accepted death, too, but as an expression of God's love more than defiance of Rome. The defiance angered Emperors and won admirers. Christianity became more prevalent in the cities of the Roman Empire, and after the Emperor Constantine had a dream telling him to put the cross on his soldiers' shields before a battle he then won; he made it the official religion of the Roman Empire in 313. People no longer had to die for their faith, but Constantine's decision was a mixed blessing. Jesus might still be Lord but Caesar owned Jesus' Church.

CREEDS

Constantine declared that there were too many kinds of Christianity, and called councils of churchmen to set up some stricter rules about what is and isn't a proper Christian idea or practice. Over the years, they produced a number of documents called *Creeds*, from the Latin word, "Credo," meaning to "to believe with one's whole heart." Easily memorized, they are still said or sung in churches today. This one, the Apostles' Creed, lists at least sixteen spiritual beliefs, as well as some essential historical details.

> I believe in God, the (1) Father almighty,
>
> (2) creator of heaven and earth. I believe in Jesus (3) Christ,
>
> (4) God's only Son, (5) our Lord,
>
> who was (6) conceived by the Holy Spirit,
>
> born of the (7) Virgin Mary,
>
> suffered under Pontius Pilate,
>
> was crucified, died, and was buried;
>
> he descended to the dead.

(8) On the third day he rose again;

(9) he ascended into heaven,

(10) he is seated at the right hand of the Father,

and (11) he will come to judge the living and the dead.

I believe in the (12) Holy Spirit,

the holy catholic church,

the (13) communion of saints,

the (14) forgiveness of sins,

the (15) resurrection of the body,

and the (16) life everlasting.

Amen.

HERESIES

The councils issued definitions of what used to be poetic ideas. Beliefs that fit the definitions were called Orthodox. *Ortho* means *straight* in Greek. Beliefs that strayed from the straight path were Heterodox or Heresy. A friend of mine points out that heresies start with a good idea, but then take it too far.

You could think of heresies like those little shoots that sometimes grow from the base of a tree. Unless you want a branch growing from there, which nobody does, you prune them off. People who believed these things were ejected from the community, unless they changed their minds. Here are some examples:

Docetism taught that Jesus was God all right, but only "seemed" to be human. He did not really suffer or die on the cross. This idea started getting popular around 100 AD, after all Jesus' friends were dead, and was officially declared a heresy in 451. The whole point of God becoming human was that he didn't fake it.

Arianism was the idea that God the Father created Jesus before creating anything else, and Jesus created the Holy Spirit after that. The orthodox view is that all three dimensions of God are infinite: they always were and always

Raphael's Transfiguration, a moment in the Gospel where Jesus reveals his Divine nature to three of his closest friends. It is also known as 'the Docetist Jesus'.

will be. The problem with Arianism is that if Jesus and the Holy Spirit are creations, even if they were first and second, they cannot be worshipped. Worshipping a created thing is idolatry. This version of Christianity became so popular it took over the church in certain countries several times between 300 and 500 CE. On the animated map, look for the yellow color starting in 325 CE, the year Arianism was declared a heresy and became a separate church.

Gnosticism was the name given to many early Christian groups who taught that only the spiritual universe is good. The material world, ruled by an evil creator, is corrupt. Sometimes the evil creator was called Satan, and sometimes called The Demiurge, but Jesus had defeated them by rising to immortality. The duty of a Christian is to progress toward the higher universe (spiritual) through philanthropy (acts of loving other human beings) and wisdom. The wisdom required to access the higher world was brought by Jesus in secret and has been passed down only to highly qualified and saintly people. Gnostic ideas kept appearing, but the councils kept declaring them heresies. Jesus had no secrets, and the world is not evil.

Marcionism followed the teachings of a Roman named Marcion who taught that the God YHWH of the Old Testament was a lesser God than the one who sent Jesus, and he deleted the Old Testament from his version of the Bible. Only the Gospel of Luke and letters of Paul measured up to his idea of a totally-loving, self-emptying God.

He denied that Jesus was really Jewish. His heresy died out after about 300 years.

As my friend said, these are good ideas taken too far…

- How could Jesus have been that good? The Docetist answer: He was so good because he wasn't really human.
- How did the Trinity get started? The Arianist answer: First God, second God's Son, and third the Holy Spirit.
- How are spiritual and material worlds related to each other? The Gnostics' answer: They are different, and one is better, therefore they are enemies.
- How could God appear so angry in one part of the Bible and so generous in another? The Marcionites' answer: The Hebrew Bible, being a human-written book, was wrong and has to be re-defined.

The papyrus is a bit of the Gospel of Peter and Marcion, one of the heretical books the church later banned. Some monk did us a favor by not burning it!

Chapter 30

Christianity: Heaven and Hell

Jesus taught that the "kingdom of heaven" was very near. He used that phrase to describe (1) a wonderful dimension of life right here on earth, (2) his second coming, and (3) life after death.

The author who made the most sense of all three meanings in my opinion was the British scholar and popular writer C. S. Lewis. He wrote the Chronicles of Narnia, and a very Narnia-like book for adults called *The Great Divorce*. It would make a great movie.

Here's the basic plot: the narrator finds himself in a gray, dreary city, and quickly learns that everyone there is dead. They come to this place from Earth, and in a few ways, it's a better place. For one thing, they live forever. For another thing, every single material possession they could ever ask for is instantly gotten: wish for a car and there it is!

Think of a bigger house and you're living in it!

But everything about the Gray City is shoddy: the clothes have holes in them, the roofs leak, the cars are rusty, even when "new." Rumors circulate that they have all been sent to Hell forever. People are mostly in bad moods, and after quarreling with their neighbors, they wish for houses further away, so suburbs sprawl to fulfill their wishes. It turns out that the things people really want—happiness, knowledge, people to love them—are not available. You can only wish for stuff, and the stuff is junk. *Maybe it is hell.*

But there is a Heaven, too, and anyone can go there. You board a flying bus with other crabby people and it takes you to a Bright Country at the top of a huge cliff. Instead of it being dusk, it's dawn up there. Instead of it being drizzly and cold, it's sunny and warm. And when you arrive in the Bright Country, you realize that you are transparent. The people up there, on the other hand, are solid.

In fact, everything is solid in Heaven. The blades of grass are hard and sharp, like the blades of a knife, on the feet of the new arrivals. Flowers look delicate, but you can't pick them or even make them budge. Apples are as hard as diamonds. The transparent people discover they are mere ghosts, doomed unless they can become solid.

Fortunately, solid people come to help, knowing in advance who's coming. A man comes to meet his former boss, to help him walk on the grass and show him how to remain in Heaven. The problem is that the solid former employee was a murderer, and the boss is outraged that a murderer is allowed into Heaven. He will not accept any help from a sinner like that. It turns out that the murderer begged for forgiveness and turned his life around, and he became solid as a result. The boss wants no part of a Heaven like that. Sinners must be punished for all time! He decides to remain a ghost and goes back to the bus.

A woman is met by a relative, and demands to see her son, who God "cruelly took from her at the age of nine." The relative says that as soon as she gives up her wish to possess and control her son again, she will start to become solid herself, and will be able to see him. The son has evolved to such a high level that he no longer comes all the way down to where the ghosts arrive. Like the boss, the woman refuses to accept the reality of Heaven. She insists that her son belongs to her and no one else.

One after another, the narrator overhears people accept or refuse help. They are willing to love or they insist on their pride. Some think Heaven is a trick designed to get them to confess secrets, but discover to their horror that there

are no secrets in the Bright Country: once you become solid, you know everything about everyone back on earth.

But the solid people also embark on a joyous outdoor life. There are talking animals, like in Narnia, and the fruit on the trees is no longer too hard and solid to eat. As you progress "from strength to strength in a life of perfect service," you move higher and higher into the mountains, where the sun seems to be ready to burst over the horizon. The great saints and even God live up there.

In short, everyone goes to Hell first, and stays there until they are ready for Heaven. They get enlightened, and solidified, and made happy, but they have to give up their sense of pride, their materialism, and their wish for separate, private lives. God damns nobody to Hell forever. He respects your free will, though. If you are not willing to say to God, "Thy will be done," then God says to you, "thy will be done," in other words, "I will not force you to come to me, to accept love and joy. I will not demand that you get over yourself and get a sense of humor. I accept your choice to remain in Hell."

The realistic thing about this fantasy is that all kinds of people seem to like Hell: there's a clergyman-ghost who lost his faith, but claims now to love asking questions more than finding answers. His solid friend who was sent to meet him tries his best to prove that heaven is not just a nice story in the Bible, but is a literal place. He says that the clergyman would have to give up all his questioning and come to terms with his shortcomings, but that God is eager to see him. But the clergyman had been famous on earth for publishing a book recommending atheism. He is still too attached to his fame and his mistaken ideas to admit his error. Hearing that there really *is* a God isn't good news for him. Nobody just "believes" in God in the Bright Country, says the solid friend. We KNOW. The narrator meets a famous author, George MacDonald, who is solid. He sums up the Great Divorce: the day has to come when joy prevails, and all the makers of misery can't spoil joy. If they want to reject the truth, so

Carved out of living rock, the orthodox churches of Lalibela are Ethiopian pilgrim destinations.

be it. And he points to a tiny crack in the earth: that crack is the "great cliff" the bus came flying up. Hell is down that crack. It's tiny, unimportant, rainy, and full of selfish little ghosts who think they are the most important people of all.

Only one solid person has ever given it up, says MacDonald: Jesus. He traded his place as Son of God to go down past Hell, past death, to Earth. He told people about the kingdom of God. Some believed, and did what they needed to do while they were alive; so when they died and got to the Grey City, and heard about the bus, of course they got on. And when they got to the Bright Country, they already knew how to forgive, and be humble, and laugh at themselves, and serve others.

Finally, we learn about God and us: God lives outside of time, and we live inside. We are free, and that's the way in which we most resemble God, so our free choice, owing to our limitations, has to happen inside of time. We can only see our own free choices through the lenses of time. If God, living outside of time, can see how our stories are going to turn out, then in Eternity, we aren't free. But inside of time, we are. We really do choose everything we do here on earth, and, if C.S. Lewis' story is right, God never stops offering us joy.

Jesus taught that the "kingdom of heaven" was very near: we can choose it now, or have it happen when Jesus returns and hope that we've made the right choices. But that day seems way off. In The Great Divorce, our freedom lasts forever: we choose our way out of Hell when we are ready. God does not keep anybody there against their will.

CHAPTER 31
Christianity: Branches On The Family Tree

Maybe the most tangled and complicated part of the religion tree is the Christian part. That might be because your author is a Christian priest, or because our country is mostly Christian, but the world's largest religion has splintered into thousands of churches, sometimes over very important differences and sometimes *not so much*.

In the last chapter, we looked at heresies of the early church, those sprouts and branches that got pruned off the tree in the first few hundred years. But the biggest branching happened when the Western and Eastern churches split. Called the Great Schism, it happened in 1054 when leaders from each side excommunicated each other. The split was a long time coming, mostly for cultural and political, not religious, reasons.

Then, five centuries later, the Protestant Reformation split the Western (not Eastern) church into many, many branches. Here are just a few:

East (Constantinople)	West (Rome)
Religious services should be conducted in the local languages	*Religious services should be conducted in Latin*
The Bishops of the five greatest Christian cities should share leadership (Alexandria, Jerusalem, Constantinople, Rome, and Antioch)	*The Bishop of Rome (Pope) is the Universal Head of the Church. The other four must obey Rome.*
Leavened bread should be used in communion	*Unleavened bread should be used in communion*
God the Father is the head of the Trinity, and the Son and Holy Spirit proceed equally from the Father	*All three persons of the blessed Trinity are equal, and none came first.*
Churches nowadays called "Orthodox" in places like Greece, Russia, Egypt, Ethiopia, Armenia, Syria, and Serbia.	*Church now called "Roman Catholic"*

1517

Lutherans, following the leadership of Martin Luther, who emphasized priesthood of all believers (not just ordained people), justification by faith alone (not by faith plus good deeds), the authority of the Bible (not traditional church teaching), and rejected the selling of indulgences, which promised admission to heaven.

1540 - 1560

Anglicans, following King Henry VIII and Elizabeth I who separated the Church of England from the Roman Catholic Church, promoted reading the Bible for everyone in English, not just for priests in Latin, and a combination of Catholic and Protestant ideas under the authority of the monarch. The king or queen would appoint new bishops to govern the church. They include the Episcopal Church in the USA (where bishops are elected by the people) and Anglicans all over the world.

1540s

Calvinists or **Reformed Protestants,** who believe that human beings are totally incapable of saving themselves. They need to rely on God's grace, proven in the sacrifice of Jesus whose death rescues the elect from their sin. God, being omniscient, knows in advance who will be saved. Communion is symbolic: there is no real presence of Christ in the bread or wine. They include Reform and Presbyterian churches today.

1600s - 1800s

Pietists, Puritans, Quakers, and **Methodists** emphasize deep spiritual experience, building communities of justice, and avoiding formal doctrines or highly-organized religion.

late 1700s

Evangelicals, who grew from several denominations in the English-speaking world, focus on individual conversion ("accepting Jesus Christ as your personal savior"), temperance (no alcohol), abolition (no slavery), less formal worship, a lesser role for clergy, and missionary work.

1800s

Unitarians emphasize the oneness of God, rather than a Trinity. Jesus is seen as a distinct and separate being from the Father.

EARLY 1900s

Pentecostals and **Charismatics** began in the US, but are now numerous in the third world. They emphasize speaking in tongues, faith-healing, converting non-believers, and the reality of miracles.

After we look at Islam, the third Abrahamic Religion, we will return (in Part Five) to two Christian churches that are even more distinctive: Mormonism and Christian Science.

CHAPTER 32

Islam: Muhammad and The Qur'an

In the beginning, the Qur'anic Voice told Muhammad, God created everything from a tiny drop of matter. The first two human beings, Adam and Eve, disobeyed with the help of The Whisperer (there's no pointy-tailed red devil in the Qur'an). But then, God gave them the chance to apologize. They swore that they would be loyal to God, and became the first Muslims.

The word Muslim means "one who surrenders, who quits fighting against God." After Adam and Eve, Noah and then Ibrahim (we know him better as Abraham) *salaamed*—made peace with—God. Ibrahim had two sons, the first with Hagar and the second with Sarah. Ishmael, the first son, according to the Qur'an, offered himself as a sacrifice if that's what God wanted. It was he, not Ibrahim, who had his faith tested.

Ishmael became the father of the 12 Arabic tribes and Isaac's son Jacob became father of the 12 Jewish tribes. Both were "muslims," the Qur'an says, because they remained faithful to the one and only God. The line of prophets included Jacob (called Yakov in the Qur'an), Joseph (Yusuf), Moses (Musa), David (Dawud), Solomon (Suleiman), John the Baptist (Yahya), Mary (Maryam), and Jesus (Isa).

According to Islam, Jesus was the holiest and most powerful of the prophets, but was not the son of God. For God, says the Qur'an, human reproduction would be too limiting. Jesus was born to the Virgin Mary according to Islam, and preached the Gospel of Love, but when the

Romans tried to crucify him, he escaped. One tradition says that Judas was crucified and died in his place as punishment for betraying him. Jesus, meanwhile, was raised into heaven to sit at God's right hand, and will one day judge the living and the dead.

Muhammad was the last of the prophets. He came to his spiritual gift late in life. He lost his mom when he was five, and he never knew his kind and well-regarded father, who died on a caravan trip before seeing his newborn son. Raised by his grandfather and uncle, both of whom died by the time he was still young, Muhammad became a sensitive, sympathetic man, rather than frightened or bitter as he might have, given so many tragedies. The angels of God, it is said, filled his heart with light, and he always looked out for people who suffered. He treated children with special kindness.

He married his employer, the wealthy widow Khadijah, who was older than he. At first, she admired him, for he made her trading business prosper without cutting corners or cheating in any way. But then they fell in love and had a very happy marriage.

In Muhammad's day, as in most desert countries today, there was not much law except for "strong beats weak." Half the adult men, if they had had resumés, would have written "raider" or "war-

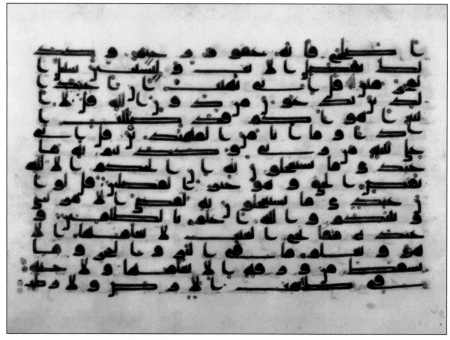

A Kufic-style page of the Quran

rior." Everything was scarce, and whoever was the fastest and strongest grabbed whatever—and whoever—they could. Slavery, oppression of women, child labor, and blood feuds were the order of the day.

Religion was not nearly strong enough to do anything about it. It was mostly polytheistic superstition, anyway. An ethical God who demanded that human beings restrain themselves and act with compassion was a weak, foreign, laughable idea. The Axial wisdom had not come to Arabia. *Yet.*

Muhammad brooded about all this suffering. He was a very religious fellow but disdained idols and drunken ceremonies. His hometown of Mecca was a sort of capital city for idolatry. In the center of the city is the cube-shaped Kaaba built by Ibrahim and Ishmael long before as a monotheistic shrine. Around the Kaaba were 360 statuettes. Each idol had one special day during the year on which pilgrims from all over the Middle East could come and beg for favors. Meccans made a lot of money selling things to pilgrim tourists, which just made Muhammad angrier.

By age 40, he was a quiet, reflective, sometimes melancholy man. He would sit in a cave outside of town and think about what life meant, and whether the cycle of trades and raids was all there was to look forward to. And then one night in the month of Ramadan, known now as The Night of Power, the angel Gabriel came to him and commanded him to listen and memorize the beginning of a poem:

"There is no god but The God.
Recite these words
in the name of God
who created humans from a drop,
who is wonderfully kind,
who teaches things to blind humanity
by the pen!"

The poetry kept coming to him over 23 years, full of God-given wisdom and instruction about religion, government, and ethics. To Muslims, the Qur'an is the greatest miracle: written down right away, word-for-word divine speech in beautiful Arabic poetry.

Unlike Jesus, Muhammad lived a long time. He got to run his new religion for many years. He not only preached and led worship, but he served as mayor of the first Muslim city (Medina) and ruler of the first Muslim state. Unlike either Buddha or Jesus, he took up the sword when attacked and sometimes before he was attacked. He married, and after Khadijah's death, took more wives. More than half these later marriages were to women of neighboring peoples and allies.

After his death, disagreement over who the successor would be turned into a split between Sunnis (the majority) and Shiites (the minority). The conflict ran deep. Blood was shed. From time to time in Muslim history, the sects cooperated, but more often they have been rivals and even enemies.

A Qur'an in the window of the Dervish House, Blagej, Bosnia & Herzegovina.

CHAPTER 33

Islam: The Religion

Muhammad had preached a simple, if not easy, religion. He instituted very few ceremonies. Like Christianity, people of any nation could join, and no baptism was required, though circumcision probably made quite a few men think twice about it. Regardless of race, language, or tribe, all were welcome if they would simply bow to the truth: a single God rules the universe, and has given his Prophet Muhammad a final, comprehensive message for all time.

There are five main duties, called the Five Pillars:

1. Formally declare your belief in the One God
2. Pray facing Mecca five times a day
3. Make a pilgrimage to Mecca once in your lifetime, unless you are too poor or ill or disabled
4. Give 2-1/2% of savings every year to the poor
5. Fast from all food, drink, and pleasures of the flesh during daylight during the lunar month of Ramadan

In addition, there are Five required Beliefs:

1. That God is One
2. That Angels are real beings, made of light, not matter, are not superior to humans, but are immortal
3. That the Qur'an is the final revealed Word of God, and the Torah, Psalms, and Gospels are earlier, less complete revelations
4. That God sent prophets throughout history, ending with Muhammad
5. That God will judge all souls on the Day of Judgment, announced by the second coming of Jesus, and will send all to heaven or hell, according to both faith and works.

All prayers face The Kaaba in Mecca

A sixth belief, common to Sunnis but not Shiites, is Predestination. the omniscient God knows everything that you are going to do. God does not cause you to do these things, because God gives us free will. We are writing the book of our lives, a page at a time, but God has already read our whole book.

Human nature is free and good. There is no Original Sin. That's a Christian idea, about the long-term effect of Adam and Eve's Fall. Instead, the Qur'an teaches, people sin because they forget they come from God. If we always remembered our divine origin, we would not be temptable by The Whisperer. We would always do the right thing. We'd be like angels, except mortal.

Islam spread like wildfire: when the land is dry, it just takes a spark. In the 600s the rivers of Christian holiness had run dry. At the time of Islam's birth, the Byzantine Empire was weak and its Christian leaders in their fine silks and jewelry were hardly the poor whom Jesus had embraced. Their Greek-speaking civilization was also weakened by wars with the other superpower of the time, Persia. When the word got out that God had finally come to the Arabs with a scripture in their own language, just as he had to Jews and Christians, the effect was electric.

The Husayn Mosque in Karbala, built on the spot which make the Sunni–Shia split final

At the time, Islam protected women's rights more than almost any religion in the world. As late as the 1800s, Muslim women were a bit ahead of women in the west. Unlike Englishwomen, they could divorce, inherit, and own large tracts of property. And they still can, but women in the secularized west now enjoy greater rights. The question of women has become a difficult one for Islam.

Compared to Christianity and Judaism, the Muslim portrait of God is different. For Jews and Christians, God can be intimately known and felt, and although holy, God is like a loving parent, sometimes even a suffering one. God loves everyone, and, according to Christians, sent his son to live and even die for everyone. The Qur'an, on the other hand, presents God as a great, wise, and compassionate master, but impossible to really know in the intimate way of Christians and Jews. The Qur'an says God does NOT love his enemies, whereas Jesus advised his followers to love everyone. It would be a mistake to say that Muslims don't pray to the same God, however, because Allah is simply the word for "the God of Abraham, Isaac, Jacob, Mary, and Jesus" in the Arabic language. Christian and Jewish people who speak Arabic (yes, there are millions!) pray to Allah, just as Spanish-speakers pray to Dios.

The Sufis are a movement within Islam who do seek an intimate parent-and-child relationship with God, and are often the easiest for westerners to relate to. The poet Rumi was a Sufi.

I mentioned Sunnis and Shiites in the last chapter: those who wanted leadership to stay in Muhammad's "house" after his death and those who wanted leaders chosen from a wider group. The Prophet's son-in law was the saintly Ali, and his "partisans" (that's what the word Shi'a or Shiite means) were sure that Muhammad had meant for Ali to rule. But a majority chose Muhammad's best friend Abu Bakr. After Abu Bakr's death, two more men would be selected before Ali finally was made the fourth Caliph (successor). The story of the split between Shiite and Sunni is fascinating, but too complicated to tell here.

It's an important story, however, because across the Middle East, especially in Lebanon, Syria, Iraq, and even as far away as Pakistan, Muslims are fighting one another in the name of "sectarianism." The split has grown deeper in recent years between Shiite (especially with the support of Iran) and Sunni (supported by Saudi Arabia and the Gulf States). It's depressingly similar to the centuries of Protestant-Catholic wars in northern Europe starting in the mid-1500s.

On the next page is a comparison of the two Muslim branches' beliefs and practices.

The niche facing Mecca in the Great Mosque, Cordoba, Spain

	Sunni (85% of world's Muslims)	Shiite (15% of world's Muslims)
History	*Sunnis say that the first of a series of successors of Muhammad were correctly chosen, by group discussion and prayer. "Caliph" means successor. The Sunni won the day and established the tradition of representative meetings to decide who would be next. Ali was finally elected as the fourth caliph, but after his assassination, the first Umayyad caliph took over and moved the capital from Ali's stronghold in Iraq to his own city, Damascus. Four great dynasties began with this fifth caliph:* **Umayyad • Abbasid • Fatimid • Ottoman**	*Shiites say that successors of Muhammad should choose who comes next, and Ali, the first man in Muhammad's family to join the faith, was intended by God to be the caliph. As Shiites kept losing the argument over succession, they gave their allegiances to twelve Imams instead, descendants of Ali and appointed by God even before they were born. The twelfth Imam, was the "Mahdi," who God took up into heaven to protect him from the jealous Sunni Caliph.*
Pillars & Beliefs	*The usual five pillars and five beliefs plus predestination*	*The usual five, plus a few more which vary by sect, and include the second coming of the hidden imam, the Mahdi*
Predestination	*Yes: emphasis on God's omniscience*	*No: emphasis on human free will*
Succession	*Should be elected by a group of wise leaders*	*Should be appointed by the Prophet himself; regarded as members of Muhammad's House and infallible spokesmen for God's will*
Intercession	*No. Pray to God directly*	*Saints, living and dead, can help carry prayers to God*
Profession of Faith	*There is only one God and Muhammad is the last prophet*	*Shiites add faith in Ali, the "friend of God"*
Ceremonies	*Usual fasting during the day and feasting at night in Ramadan, and two great feasts (Eid)*	*Same, plus commemoration of the martyrdom of Husayn by Sunni Caliph Yazid I. Shiites have many more pilgrimage sites in addition to Mecca.*

PART FIVE

Newer Branches

This last section covers the last five hundred years. We'll start with Sikhism, which updated and combined Hinduism and Islam beginning in the 1500s. During the 1800s hundreds of new religions sprung up in New England which were truly American. They focused on the power of the individual and shone with the optimism of a frontier culture. Shakers, Seventh-Day Adventists, Mormons, Christian Science, and Unitarians are examples, but also astrology, mesmerism, homeopathy, the Transcendentalism of Emerson and Thoreau, and nutrition science. In this book, we focus on just two: Mormon Christianity and Christian Science.

The Baha'i Faith grew in Persia in the 1800s from thoroughly Muslim roots, but embraced other religions in a very modern way, with the goal of including, rather than replacing, earlier revelations. Ahmadiyya Islam grew up in India in the 1800s, with a Muslim leader combining his faith with Christianity and Buddhism. People describe America as a melting-pot of cultures, but India has been doing it for a lot longer. We finish our tour of the newest branches of the Tree of World Religions with a look at another hybrid, born in the Caribbean with longing for Mother Africa: Rastafarianism.

In Part Five, the tree metaphor doesn't work as well, because on a real tree, branches split off from one another like new species evolving, and never grow back together like many of the religions in this section.

CHAPTER 34

Sikhism: History & Theology

Hinduism has always been the dominant religion in India, but starting in the 1200s a powerful Muslim civilization conquered most of the subcontinent. A minority joined the new monotheistic religion, but in the early 1500s, a teacher (guru) named Nanak appeared who combined what he believed was the best of Hinduism AND Islam. He called his followers "sikhs," which means "students," a humble name if there ever was one. By the way, "Taliban" means the "students" in Arabic, which just illustrates what people can do with perfectly good words.

Nanak was born in the countryside near Lahore, Pakistan. His parents were of the merchant caste, and they arranged a marriage for him according to Hindu dharma. He practiced both the chanting and river-baths of Hindu bhakti yoga and the careful study of the classics of both Hinduism (jnana yoga) and Islam.

One day at age thirty, he didn't come back from meditating in the river, and his family was very worried. Three days later, he returned, but remained mysteriously silent for a day. Everyone was relieved at his safety but mystified by his silence. Had he seen a god? A ghost? An angel? As it turned out, he had seen The God, the Creator of All. God had given him a cup of heavenly nectar, and asked him to share this experience with others. God didn't explain exactly what heaven was, or what nectar symbolized, or which "others" Nanak was supposed to teach, but as the years passed, he found many ways to teach the oneness of God, the nourishment of God, and our need for gratitude to God. Nanak had seen what's on the other side of the veil that separates the material world from the spiritual one.

Most religions are based on powerful experiences like these. Words are just words, but BEING in the heavenly presence changes everything. Think of Mary. Or Paul. Or Moses. Or Muhammad. Nanak became a full-time traveling guru, more or less jumping to stage four in Hinduism, though he didn't call himself a Hindu any more. He didn't call himself a Muslim, either. He went to Mecca, where Muslims tried to get him to convert, and to Baghdad, where he argued for hours with the professors in the Islamic universities. He visited holy shrines and praised God there, and the people who met him were impressed at how he seemed to radiate love.

But he wasn't just a nice holy man. He was a rebel, too. He was doing bathing meditation at dawn with Hindu priests (brahmins) one morning, and they began throwing water toward the rising sun, offering prayers to their dead ancestors. He started throwing it in the opposite direction, towards his home country. When they asked him why, he said, "if you can give water to your dead ancestors in heaven, surely I can send it to my fields in the Punjab." His religion was not going to be supernatural. A good example of this was what he did with the idea of "nectar." Instead of singing songs about how God metaphorically feeds all his children, Sikh temples would serve actual meals to anyone who came. They would also provide places of rest for any visitors. Even today, the gurdwara is as much banquet-hall as church, and many of them let you spend the night, like an inn or hostel.

Nanak didn't intend to start a whole new religion. He felt comfortable in both Hinduism and Islam. On his deathbed, he asked them to cover him with a white burial cloth and leave flowers on either side of him. Then he sent them away, with the agreement that whichever group's flowers did not wilt could have his body. The Hindus planned cremation and the Muslims planned burial. In the morning, the body was gone and both Hindu and Muslim flowers looked perfectly fresh! Who knows what happened? (Nowadays, most Sikhs cremate their dead, by the way.) Following his death came a series of nine more gurus to lead the community.

The fifth guru, Arjan, is best known for two things:

Every copy of the Adi Granth is identical to the original

1. Compiling the Adi Granth, the Holy Scripture of Sikhism, a collection of wisdom from the era of the first five gurus, and

2. building the Golden Temple in the city of Amritsar. Unlike Hindu Temples with only one door, the Sikh Temple had doors on all four sides, symbolizing that the new religion would be open to people from all cultures, and from all four of the Indian castes. It is surrounded by a huge outdoor pool called The Tank, used for sacred bathing rituals. Like all Sikh houses of worship, the Golden Temple has a very active ministry feeding 100,000 people a day. If you ever visit, you'll be most welcome to walk all around and have some delicious food.

The tenth guru, Guru Gobind Singh, was best known for proclaiming the Adi Granth as the final guru. Gurus one through ten had been human beings. Number eleven is a book.

This allowed the religion to grow worldwide. No longer did you need to live near the great teacher or make a long trip to hear him speak. The book was copied and placed in every gurdwara.

Some of the most important teachings in the Adi Granth are:

- God is One, True, and Present; the Sustainer and Creator of all things; without fear or hatred. God is not subject to time, has no form, no birth, and no death. God is self-revealing and full of grace.

- Humans are too self-centered. We think we can do everything on our own. We are too proud. The word for this is "haumai," the human insistence of making it on our own, rather than depending on God. Scripture says haumai leads to lust, anger, greed, and pride.

- Humans are ignorant, and need teaching. God is the Great Guru. Learning helps us see the connections which the ignorant cannot see. Seeing Creation and the hand of the Creator helps reconnect us with the deepest truths in the universe.

- Ignorance and haumai together keep humans trapped in samsara. Like Hindus, Sikhs believe in reincarnation. Muslims do not.
- Grace is freely given by God, who speaks to us in infinite love. Past lives determine the nature of our birth, but grace gets us out of the samsara trap.
- Salvation is reunification with God; and just as the Buddha said Nirvana can be reached in any lifetime, Sikhs also reject the Hindu idea that a person has to work their way up to the top caste and the fourth stage to achieve moksha. It's not just our works that save us, say the gurus, but God's grace. In this way, Sikhism is very close to Christianity.

A Sikh pilgrim at the Golden Temple in Amritsar, India

CHAPTER 35

Sikhism: Daily Life

Sikhism tries to help a person find God within, not outside or far away. But their religion is not private. It revolves around the house of worship, the gurdwara. Any place with a copy of the Adi Granth is a gurdwara, and the book—always beautifully-bound and always identical, page-for-page, to the original—is cushioned and canopied in its place of honor.

Sikh worship happens frequently, and holidays can occur on any day of the week. You must take a bath or shower right before coming. The service always includes singing, a reading from scripture, and a story about one of the gurus. Many other things, modern or traditional, could be included: a film, a dance, stories from literature, or reciting poetry. The service always ends with eating a special holy communion cake together.

The gurdwara also has a kitchen, and everyone helps prepare, serve, and clean up. The meal is an essential part of the worship. Neighbors, the poor, travelers, and friends are always invited, and lots of extra food is always prepared. Everyone sits on the floor, regardless of social status.

Once a young Sikh reaches 14 years old, he or she can become a baptized adult, and is then responsible for the 5 K's.

Volunteers help in the giant gurdwara kitchen

1. **Kara:** iron wrist guards, to remind the wearer that your hands are always to do God's work.

2. **Kaccha:** a pair of shorts, originally worn by soldiers, who had to be ready at a moment's notice to jump into a fight. They are worn only under clothes by women, but men may wear them as work clothes on hot summer days.

3. **Kirpan:** a symbolic sword, reminder of the duty to defend the weak.

4. **Kangha:** a comb to symbolize tidiness in contrast with some Hindu holy people who grow dreadlocks as a sign of disdain for worldly vanity.

5. **Kesh:** uncut hair for both men and women, kept in a crown-like turban by men. Women are free to tie, braid, wrap, and so on.

Sikh ethical duties include

1. giving 1/10 of one's income to charity
2. speaking truthfully. "As honest as a Sikh" is a compliment in India.
3. defending one's religion and the rights of others to practice theirs'. Sikhs often volunteer for the military, and their courage is legendary.
4. eating only meat that has been properly slaughtered
5. avoiding sex outside of marriage
6. avoiding using tobacco
7. making no distinction based on caste, color, language, or creed

A little girl prays at the Golden Temple

In the 2002 romantic comedy *Bend it Like Beckham*, a young Sikh woman becomes a terrific soccer player, but hides it from her parents, who would disapprove. In the end, however, her father decides to let her compete (despite her mother's protests that the uniform is not modest enough) because it is important for a person to fight for the right to do their best. Sikhs are not embarrassed that their turbans and swords make them stand out in a crowd. Their religion has a good reputation all over the world, and they try to uphold it. After the September 11, 2001 terrorist attacks, many American Sikhs were mistaken for Muslims, but they did not get angry about it. They used it as a teaching opportunity: 'we aren't Muslims,' they said, 'but we stand with them: what the hijackers did was not Muslim, either.'

Bend it Like Beckham

CHAPTER 36

Mormon Christianity

Mormonism is a truly American reboot of Christianity, having begun in upstate New York during that great century of creative spirituality, the 1800s. The official name is the Church of Jesus Christ of Latter-Day Saints. The scriptures of the LDS Church are the Christian Bible and the Book of Mormon, named after an ancient American prophet named Mormon. He said he was a member of the Nephite people, one of four tribes who emigrated from Ancient Israel around 600 BC.

The Book of Mormon describes these tribes building ships and bringing their faith to America. The first ones came from the House of Joseph, and later arrivals were from the Tribe of Judah. Later on, Jesus himself came to these Native Americans and taught them his Gospel. Modern Mormons are each members of one of the 12 tribes of Israel, and receive their tribal identification from a patriarchal blessing, a once-in-a-lifetime prophecy that reveals to a person his/her deep spiritual gifts and a clue to the challenges they will face later in life.

The arrivals of the Jewish tribes and Jesus, unknown to history, were discovered by Joseph Smith in his early twenties after he was visited by God the Father and Jesus. Somewhat later, the angel Moroni (son of the Native American prophet Mormon) came to show him a place where he would find priceless wisdom, and there he dug, and found gold plates, engraved in an ancient language, with the revelations which became the Book of Mormon. The angel taught him how to read them, and he translated them into English. Smith was himself a very charismatic mystic, a person with powerful insight into the meanings of things, and not afraid to describe the mysteries he believed in. His assassination in 1844 by a lynch mob ended his run for the US Presidency and established him as a martyr in the persecuted church.

The Mormons left their settlements in Illinois and then Missouri shortly thereafter and headed for Utah, where they established a government with no

Joseph Smith

separation of church and state. Brigham Young took over from Smith and led the church and state until 1877 in a utopian experiment in frontier settlement and faith.

Until late in that century, polygamy was part of the religion, which caused much friction with civil authorities. Polygamy was officially halted in 1890, though a few small fringe groups of Mormons still allow "plural marriage" in isolated areas of the west.

In pioneering this new religion, Smith and his followers tried to restore what they saw as the faith of Jesus' own time as well as the innovations worked out by the tribes that came to this hemisphere and were wiped out by war during Moroni's lifetime. Writing the plates recording God's work in the New World (600 BC to 400 AD) was Moroni's final act. So Mormonism is old as well as new.

Joseph Smith's religious innovations include these:

- There are prophets in the modern age (such as Joseph Smith and Brigham Young)

- There is no Original Sin. In fact, there is an Original Blessing: humans are created by Heavenly Father and are taught right and wrong. When we are born, we enter mortal life where our task is to practice living according to God's will.

- After death, people go to the spirit world to wait for resurrection. Those who did God's Will go on to the Celestial Kingdom. Those who fought God or sinned greatly are relegated to the Telestial Kingdom. Neutral souls go to the Terrestrial Kingdom. But these are all heavenly places, far happier than earth.

- In the long run, people are capable of becoming divine. There is no limit to our perfectibility, because we are literally, not just metaphorically, children of God.

Salt Lake City Temple

The LDS Faith also brings back the pre-Axial spirit of supernatural mystery. Mormons say that when those ancient tribes came to America, they brought ceremonies with them, and Mormonism therefore has "ordinances" not found in other Christian churches:

Endowment, which teaches people how to signal to the angels guarding heaven's gates that they have been prepared for important heavenly roles. Endowment requires a person to wear sacred garments under their clothing for the rest of their lives. Missionaries must have endowment beforehand, and most higher levels of church responsibility require it. Observers find similarities in the Temple Endowment Rites to certain rituals of the Masons.

Priesthood is different in the LDS Church from other Christian denominations, and different from ancient Judaism. Priesthood is given at age twelve to males who show virtue in their beliefs and daily actions. As they gets older, they can receive certain church offices, including Apostle, Elder, Patriarch, and High Priest.

Eternal Marriages, performed by a person with priesthood authority, which assure the couple and their future children of being together in heaven. Instead of "till death do us part," they vow "for time and all eternity." The seal cannot be removed by civil divorce, but can be cancelled in the Temple.

Baptism For The Dead, in which a living person receives baptism on behalf of someone who has died. The LDS Church teaches that the dead person in heaven has the choice to accept or reject this baptism. Once again, this idea seems new to other Christians, but it is not: Baptism For The Dead existed for a short while in a few early Christian churches in the Roman Empire until the Catholic Church declared it heresy.

Mormon culture, especially in the states around the LDS Church's center in Utah, includes a number of distinctive features:

- **Tithing,** giving 10% of your income to the Church, which virtually every Mormon practices.
- **Family Home Evenings,** in which everyone is home for dinner, scripture study, discussion, music, and treats; usually on Monday nights.
- **Avoiding Impurity,** such as sex outside marriage, tattoos, piercings, alcohol, and caffeine, all based on the idea of keeping the body pure.
- **The Mission.** It is an honor and sought-after privilege to go on a Mission, almost always overseas, in pairs. Missionaries, usually before college, spread the Gospel of Jesus of Latter-Day Saints with energy and enthusiasm, and are expected to be shining examples of the wholesome life which comes from living the Gospel. 75% of missionaries are men ages 19-26. They work six-hour days and begin saving for their mission when they are in elementary school, because missionaries pay their entire way for two years. In 2015, there were 74,000 missionaries at 418 missions around the world.
- **A hierarchy of offices** within the ward (local church) and stake (region). These offices have duties and require increasing spiritual devotion. The head of each ward is the Bishop, and each stake has a President. At the top of the hierarchy is a President, believed to also be a Prophet, assisted by two counselors and a council of twelve apostles, in imitation of Jesus' leadership team.
- **No professional clergy,** although church leaders are sometimes paid "housing allowances." Leadership is normally regarded as a gift to the community, rather than a paid career.

The American Dream says *anyone can succeed by working hard*, so Mormonism is very American. It's a pioneer religion, a religion of hard work and devotion to family life. It's optimistic, even to the point of souls perfecting themselves long after death. But there is a dark side to the American Dream, too: there were people here when the colonists and immigrants arrived—the Indians. Being a pioneer religion, the LDS church clashed with Indians and, despite the presence of Native Americans in their scriptures, they have not been particularly successful in converting them. The other major group excluded from the American Dream—enslaved Africans and their descendants—have only belatedly and imperfectly been brought into the American Dream, and their path to acceptance into the Latter Day Saints has been rocky as well. The church disavowed its past teachings about black inferiority in a statement in December, 2013 that stopped short of apologizing for barring African Americans from priesthood before 1978.

Mormons on mission

CHAPTER 37

The Baha'i Faith

Around the same time Joseph Smith was heading west with his Mormon Pioneers, a young man named Bahaullah joined a new faith, too: the Babi Shiites were followers of a new Persian messiah who called himself The Gate, and predicted that someone would come soon to unify all humanity and end religious wars. As usual, the religious leaders of the Persian Empire declared The Gate a heretic, and had him assassinated. The dead man's followers planned revenge, though one of them, the young nobleman Bahaullah objected loudly and in writing. The plotters were discovered and executed, and Bahaullah was tossed in the most awful dungeon imaginable, the Black Pit. His prayers there led him not to despair, but to a deep sense of peace and trust in God. Freed with the help of the Russian Ambassador, he was exiled to Baghdad, in the Ottoman Empire.

For the next twenty years, he became a respected teacher of Sufis, Shiites, and Sunnis, and sketched the outlines of a new united religion of the world: Baha'i. Unfortunately, the Ottomans didn't like the new religion any more than the Persians did, and tried to get his help in cracking down on other followers of The Gate. He refused, which landed him in a military prison in Acre, in the Ottoman province of Palestine (now Israel). Despite this, he continued teaching and meditating, and came to believe he was not a mere teacher but the latest Manifestation of God.

According to Bahaullah, God has shown himself in many persons over the centuries: Abraham, Moses, Jesus, Muhammad, Krishna, Buddha, Rama, Zoroaster, and others. Each brought knowledge and wisdom to earth appropriate for their time and place. Bahaullah specifically said he was NOT the final manifestation: God will surely send more in the future. His teachings still sound very modern, 150 years after Bahaullah's death:

- racism of any kind is wrong. Race is a human invention, not a divine creation. Science has confirmed this revelation over and over again through DNA research.
- males and females must be equal in all areas, and thus the next Manifestation of God might well be female.
- science is not the enemy of religion. When science discovers something, religion ought to incorporate it.
- there should be a world government and a world language. (So far, not much progress).
- there should be no clergy in the new religion, and Baha'is should be democratic, which they are.
- Houses of Worship should be open to all, have nine sides, extensive gardens, and a dome.

1. Wilmette, Illinois – 1953
2. Sydney, Australia – 1961
3. Kampala, Uganda – 1962
4. Frankfurt, Germany – 1964
5. Panama City, Panama – 1972
6. Apia, Samoa – 1984
7. New Delhi, India – 1986
8. Santiago, Chile – under construction

The very first House was in Ashkabad, Turkmenistan – completed 1908, damaged by an earthquake in 1948, and then torn down in 1962 by the anti-religion Soviet government. If the success of a religion which hopes to unite the world can be measured by the reactions it provokes, The Baha'i Faith is very successful.

There are 5-7 million of them worldwide, fewer than the number of Jews, but in many countries in the Muslim world, membership is a crime.

The Lotus Temple in New Delhi

CHAPTER 38

Christian Science

The other hopeful American-born religion we'll look at came some decades later. In 1875, Mary Baker Eddy wrote *Science and Health With A Key To The Scriptures*, the founding book of Christian Science. Like the Mormons, the church was to have no ordained clergy. Unlike the LDS Church, Christian Science has no sacraments, statues, seminaries or hierarchy. Christian Science was to be a modern, democratic church in tune with the times. If Mormonism includes a lot of Pre-Axial mysteries, Christian Science embraces the rationality of the Axial Age thinkers so long ago.

Mary Baker Eddy insisted, with many of her anti-materialist friends of the time, that humans are not physical beings on a spiritual journey. We are spiritual beings on a physical journey. This goes back to Plato: MIND is supreme, not MATTER. "There is no life, truth, intelligence, nor substance in matter," she wrote in *Science and Health*. "All is infinite Mind and its infinite manifestation, for God is All-in-all. Spirit is immortal Truth; matter is mortal error. Spirit is the real and eternal; matter is the unreal and temporal. Spirit is God, and man is His image and likeness. Therefore man is not material; he is spiritual."

Because of this, she reasoned, most sickness is caused by mistaken beliefs. Sometimes you are aware of them, and sometimes they are unconscious. Thinking through your beliefs with the help of a healer can cure most sicknesses. She called it "Christian *Science*" because Science is the least superstitious way of knowing. The original meaning of "science" was "knowledge." It's only recently that the word has come to mean "something proven experimentally."

Her ideas about God fit with this worldview: God is not a person who loves, God IS love. Not the giver of life, but life itself. We don't die, we just readjust to another level of existence to which our mind goes. There is no final judgment. Jesus was not God or one of the gods, but was the first person to fully manifest

MARY BAKER G. EDDY,
The Discoverer and Founder of Christian Science.

112

the Divine Mind which we all can have, with training. Having such a disciplined mind made Jesus the supreme "knower" (scientist) of his day. He showed the way, by showing what God knows: *death is an illusion of the flesh.* Christian Scientists also regard God as metaphorically both male and female, and Mrs. Eddy's Lord's Prayer began, "Father-Mother God, all-harmonious."

Her friend and student C. Lulu Blackman described this remarkable woman: "When she entered the classroom ... she made her way to a slightly raised platform, turned and faced us. She wore an imported black satin dress heavily beaded with tiny black jet beads, black satin slippers, beaded, and had on her rarely beautiful diamonds. ... She stood before us, seemingly slight, graceful of carriage, and exquisitely beautiful even to critical eyes. Then, still standing, she faced her class as one who knew herself to be a teacher by divine right. ... She turned to the student at the end of the first row of seats and took direct mental cognizance of him, plainly knocked at the door of (his) consciousness. It was as if a question had been asked, and

The Mother Church of Christ, Scientist in Boston

answered, and a benediction given. Then her eyes rested on the next in order and the same recognition was made. This continued until each member of the class had received the same mental cognizance. No audible word voiced the purely mental contact."

She was frequently ill in childhood, and this experience made her think deeply about the source and remedy of illness. She discovered the power of faith healing in her own life, and applied herself to experiments with others to extend her theories. Christian Science Practitioners are licensed by the church to counsel people, encouraging them to use the power of their mind to heal illness. Broken bones and crooked teeth, being purely physical, may be fixed by surgeons and orthodontists, but conditions like diabetes, high blood pressure, the flu, and even cancer are claimed to be curable with prayer.

Christian Science hit its peak in the 1930s, when the Mother Church in Boston's Back Bay was built. Reading Rooms and Churches were built across the country and the world, and membership reached its peak of 270,000. Seventy years later, numbers were down to about 100,000.

CHAPTER 39

Ahmadiyya Islam

In the 1880s, around the same time Mrs. Eddy was developing Christian Science, another branch of Islam sprouted, this time in India. The founder was a Shi'ite named Mirza Ghulam Ahmad, and like Mrs. Eddy, he was a reformer.

As a Muslim, Ahmad believed that Muhammad was a prophet and the Qur'an was God's word. He performed the five pillars, and unlike fanatics then and now, he taught only nonviolent resistance to their British and Hindu oppressors. "Jihad," he reminded Muslims, means struggle. The inner struggle to purify yourself is more important than any outer struggle to defend Islam. Very few so-called "holy wars" were really holy, he said, so Muslims should not resort to violence. Ahmadiyyas were active in the American Civil Rights Movement in the 1950s and 1960s.

Ahmadiyya Mosque in Calgary

But unlike his fellow Muslims, he didn't think that Muhammad and the Qur'an were the last word. He declared himself the Mahdi, a Shiite saint taken to heaven by God and hidden from his pursuers in 874 CE (see chart on p. 112). The Mahdi is the Promised Messiah who will usher in the End Times, along with Jesus. Ahmad tried to unite all religions.

To Hindus, he said, 'when you teach that Gods like Vishnu incarnate as human beings, you are not right. Those avatars, like Krishna and the Buddha, who you think are gods in human form, are just prophets. I am one, too.'

To Buddhists, he said, 'you teach that everyone can become enlightened, and following the eightfold path is the way to get there. My path is the same, so let's walk together. You could even call me a Buddha.'

To Christians, he said, 'Jesus taught that he would come again to judge the living and the dead. Well, that time has come! And furthermore, as we Muslims already know, Jesus didn't die on the cross. Jesus escaped, travelled to India seeking the Lost Tribes of Israel, and lived with holy men who immediately recognized him as an enlightened being. Jesus died at a ripe old age.'

Ahmad made friends with Christian pastors, Muslim imams, Hindu gurus, and Buddhist lamas. In 1888, he founded his reform movement that now bears his name: Ahmadi or Ahmadiyya. His disciples called him the fulfillment of ALL religious hopes, the Mahdi.

Just as the Jews needed Jesus 1400 years after Moses, Islam needed Ahmad 1400 years after Muhammad. Religions had become too wrapped up in laws and conflicts, and need to return to the basic message. Jesus was not the Son of God, and Ahmad was not The Prophet. They were just reformers.

Here's a sad irony: remember how, after the death of Muhammad, the Shiites believed that future leaders ought to come from the family of Muhammad and the Sunnis believed that leaders ought to be elected by a council? After the death of Ahmad, his followers split over the same issue.

You can find Ahmadiyya Mosques all over the world.

- Their mosque in Copenhagen has a beautiful spherical dome. It's named after Ahmad's wife, Nusrat Jehan, the "Mother of the Faithful."
- Their mosque in London, "House of Victories" is dignified and simple.
- Their mosque in Calgary, Alberta makes use of silver on the dome, and a single prayer-tower or minaret. It's called the "House of Light."

Ahmadiyyas describe themselves as outgoing, modern Muslims, but their opponents, most notably the governments of Saudi Arabia and Pakistan, call them heretics and infidels. Ahmadi places of worship there can't even be called "mosques." They are well-known internationally for building hospitals, running schools, running development projects in the poorest places on earth, and for hurrying to provide relief from floods and earthquakes.

The Ahmadiyya motto is "Love for all, hatred for none."

Two girls in an Ahmadiyya school in Sierra Leone, Africa

CHAPTER 40

Rastafari

Among the most famous and least understood new religions of the Americas is the Afrocentric faith called Rastafari. Outsiders, trying to make it sound like other religions, often call it "Rastafarianism," but people following this way of life don't. It was founded in Jamaica in the 1930s, and is popular all over the Caribbean among the descendants of enslaved Africans. "Ras" was the title of Haile Selassie I, who was emperor of Ethiopia from 1930 to 1974, and "Tafari" was his first name given by his parents before he took the throne. Selassie is believed to have descended from the Queen of Sheba and King Solomon of Israel and Judah.

Rastafari thus focus their faith on Selassie himself, who they take to be a second coming of Christ. He was the only monarch of the only country in Africa not to be colonized, and this gave him great prestige. They accept Christian and Jewish scriptures, and believe that God came to earth in Ethiopia as a blessing to that country for its long Christian history. They refer to God by his Biblical name, Jah, which is short for Jehovah, which is a possible pronunciation of the ancient name YHWH. They believe that Jah

Lion of Judah monument in Addis Abba, Ethiopia, commemorating Selassie's descent

calls all African people back to the motherland, Ethiopia, to build the Kingdom of Zion there. Zion is also a name for Jerusalem, the most sacred city in Judaism and site of Jesus' death and resurrection. The African Zion will stand as a rebuke to the values of the world, such as oppression, materialism, violence, and colonization. Its capital will be the ancient Christian shrine of Lalibela, the Ethiopian Orthodox church pictured earlier in this book, carved out of the living pink rock in the shape of a cross.

As part of their utopia—their heaven on earth—Rastafari use cannabis as their sacred herb, smoking it in ceremonies for the peaceful intoxication it provides. They follow a strict kosher or vegetarian diet. They wear dreadlocks as a symbol of their "dread" of God's terrible judgment of this world's sinfulness. Dreads are worn in the spirit of the Biblical hero Samson, whose great strength was a gift from God in return for his mother promising to raise him to avoid strong drink, sexual relationships, and haircuts. A nazirite was dedicated to the service of God and set apart by these three vows. The Rastafari emulate only Samson's hair vow.

Haile Selassie

Like the prophets of the Bible who criticized "Babylon" as a city of godlessness, Rastafari use the name Babylon to refer to people, especially Europeans, who exploit others, who use the media for propaganda, who took Africans to be slaves in the New World, and who do not value the natural world except as a storehouse of resources to be taken. "Babylon" also refers to police, especially when they take bribes, and to corrupt politicians.

- They have a special vocabulary, which is ever-changing, and sometimes very fun:
- "Jah," the one God: Father, Son, and Holy Spirit
- "I and I" meaning "me," because people should be subjects, not objects. It can also, in context, mean "we"
- "Politricks" instead of "politics"
- "Overstanding" instead of "understanding," because learning should elevate you
- "Queen" for "wife" or "girlfriend," as in the Biblical Queen of Sheba, who came from Ethiopia
- "Zion" meaning Ethiopia or Africa, once the Day of Judgment happens
- "Cool Runnings" meaning have a safe journey

- "Lion" meaning a great person, a powerful soul, a righteous man
- "One Love" an expression of farewell, a promise of unity
- "Livication" instead of "dedication," for obvious reasons. Kind of a pun
- The most famous Rastafari was the Jamaican reggae singer Bob Marley, whose music included the hits "Exodus," "Africa Unite, "Buffalo Soldier," and "Redemption Song," all full of religious and pan-African imagery.

Bob Marley

Epilogue

Will religions keep on branching, or might the process change? So far, it looks as if religion gets more and more diverse as time goes on. Like the branches of the tree, spreading toward the sun, it appears that our faiths will keep on differentiating. From Hinduism comes Buddhism, and then different kinds of Buddhism. And Christian churches just keep on splintering.

But just because that's how things have been going does not mean they'll keep on branching out. In fact, there's another metaphor: the river. Rivers happen when streams come together, flowing from higher to lower places. Rivers find each other on the way to the sea, one tributary adding to another until the majestic main stream merges with the ocean itself, the Lowest Place, following the Dao.

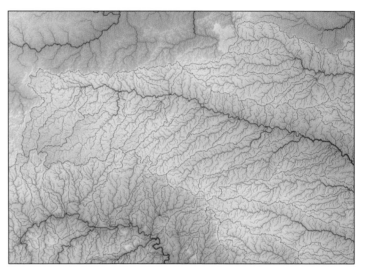

Tributaries of the Wonderfully-Named "Rio Madre De Dios" in Peru

The way we've been telling the story in this course makes religion look like a tree branching from root to leaf. But, a river system looks a lot like a tree.

What if the branches of religion are more like a river's, growing slowly together instead of apart, finding common ground, merging into a single stream? What if, sometime in the future, all the separate symbols and stories are discovered to be just variations on a single great spiritual unity? What if the paths to God all lead downstream to an ocean of truth, and the wisdom turns out to be singular, not plural?

Too hard to imagine? Well, step back. What if the Big Bang was not the first time a universe started? What if the ancient Hindu scriptures are right, and this universe is not the only one? What if the expansion from Creation as we know it has been followed, many times, by a contraction? What if bangs only last so long, to be replaced by everything falling back together until the universe contracts into an infinitely tiny mass? What do you call "bang" in reverse, "gnab"?

What if, in other words, we're so used to the differentiation phase that we cannot imagine an integration phase? What if we live in the era of centrifugal force, and there is an era to come of centripetal force?

For the moment, a tree book makes more sense than a river book. But we might be wrong. Unity and Diversity are *both* sacred. Coming from the One and moving toward the One are *both* true:

Siddhartha found infinity under a tree and Jesus affirmed infinity after being nailed to one.

The rivers of India rise in the cold Himalayas and flow with the Eternal Dao to the Sea from which all species emerged.

The Reach of World Religions

Pink Orthodox Christianity
Light Purple Protestant Christianity
Dark Purple Catholic Christianity
Light Green Sunni Islam
Dark Green Shia Islam
Medium Green Other Islam
Orange Hinduism
Red Buddhism, Daoism, Confucianism, and Shinto

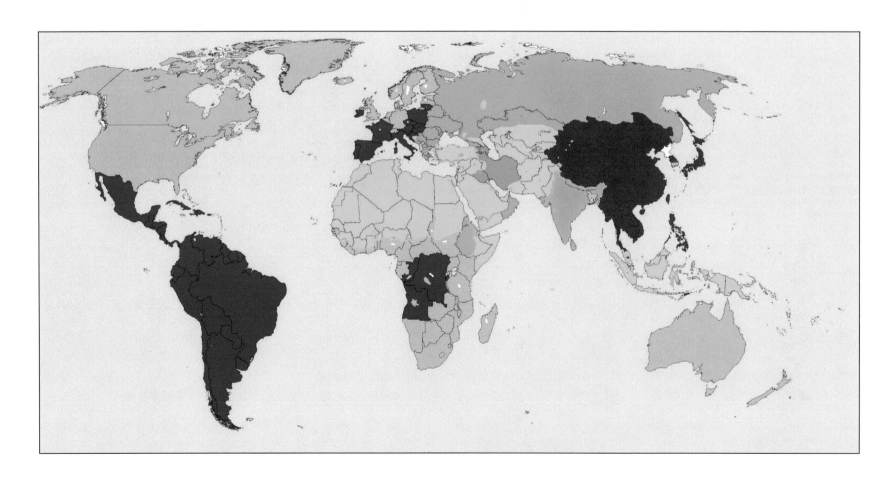

Citations & Credits

Chapter 1, Older and Newer

Page 2 Karen Armstrong, *The History of God, Random House, 2011 edition.*

Page 2 Goddess figurines http://www.dailymail.co.uk/sciencetech/article-1212320/Ancient-figurines-toys-mother-goddess-statues-say-experts-9-000-year-old-artefacts-discovered.html

Chapter 2, Higher and Lower

Page 4 Night sky http://en.wikipedia.org/wiki/File:Starry_Night_at_La_Silla.jpg

Page 5 Great Chain of Being Image "Traditional Worldview" by Brigitte Parenteau based on Great Chain of Being in E.F. Schumacher's *Guide For The Perplexed*. San Francisco: Harper Perennial, 1977.

Page 6 Skin cell http://commons.wikimedia.org/wiki/File:Skin_surface (human).jpg

Chapter 3, What do we know, and how do we know it?

Page 7 Flashlight allegory comes from Huston Smith, "Another World To Live In," Mark Jurgensmyer, ed. *Teaching The Introductory Course In Religion*, Chapel Hill: Scholars' Press, 1991.

Page 7 At night in the forest http://www.dorcydirect.com/p-438-41-0435-metal-gear-xl-m-extreme-618-lumen-led-flashlight.aspx. Permission from Dorcy Direct.

Page 8 Chart adapted from John Meagher's *The Truing of Christianity*, New York: Doubleday, 1990

Chapter 4, Theisms and Atheisms

Page 11 Big Rock http://www.background-free.com/landscapes/desert/big_rock_in_desert.jpg.html

Chapter 5, Defining Religion

Page 13 Elephant http://www.flickr.com/photos/exfordy/429417273

Page 14 Dalai Lama http://commons.wikimedia.org/wiki/File:Happiness.The_Dalai_Lama_at_Vancouver.jpg

Chapter 6, Comparing Religions

Page 16 Ninian Smart, *Secular Education and the Logic of Religion*, New York: Humanities Press, 1968

Chapter 7, Indigenous Religions

Page 17 Mbuti boy, http://cdn29.us1.fansshare.com/pictures/congo/pygmee-tjej-epulu-congo-rainforest-1260394580.jpg

Page 18 Australian Aboriginal Dreamtime from the video http://www.youtube.com/watch?v=H7oE4sKIDuU

Page 19 Diagram of Kongo Cosmology by the author, from his classroom wall.

Chapter 8, Creation Stories Comparison Project

Page 20 Hebrew Cosmology of the Universe, from American Academy of Religion http://www.aarweb.org/syllabus/syllabi/g/gier/306/commoncosmos.htm

Page 21 Manoomin from http://commons.wikimedia.org/wiki/File:Wild_rice_harvesting_19th_century.jpg

Chapter 9, Hinduism: The Gods

Page 24 Swastika on temple in Tibet from http://en.wikipedia.org/wiki/Swastika

Page 25 Hindu Temple in Maple Grove, MN by the author

Chapter 10, Hinduism: The Four Wants

Page 26 Smith, Huston, *The World's Religions*, Harper-Collins, 1998

Page 26 Om http://mandalachakra.wordpress.com/tag/agni/ Permission requested 4/1/14

Page 27 Sadhu following Vishnu http://upload.wikimedia.org/wikipedia/commons/7/73/%28A%29_Sadhu_in_Varanasi%2C_India.jpg

Chapter 11, Hinduism: Four Stages, Four Castes, Four Paths

Page 28 Woman praying in the Ganges at Varanasi http://deliraradois.blogspot.com/2011_09_01_archive.html

Page 29 Gandhi http://commons.wikimedia.org/wiki/Mohandas_K._Gandhi

Page 30 Amarath comic book cover http://en.wikipedia.org/wiki/List_of_Amar_Chitra_Katha_comics

Chapter 12 The Greek Pantheon

Page 32 Greek goddesses on temple pillars from personal collection

Chapter 13, Norse Gods and Goddesses

Page 34 Ymir

Chapter 14, Maya Polytheism

Page 36 http://commons.wikimedia.org/wiki/File:Mayan_-_Dwarf_Figurine_-_Walters_20092036_-_Detail_A.jpg

Page 37 Gods and planets from Popol Vuh cover art https://itunes.apple.com/us/book/popol-vuh/id665701817?mt=11

Page 38 Pyramid at Tikal, Guatemala by the author

Chapter 15, Zoroastrian Dualism

Page 39 Fire-temple http://latimesphoto.files.wordpress.com/2011/09/la-0912-pin12.jpg

Page 40 Kaaba or Cube of Zoroaster http://commons.wikimedia.org/wiki/File:Ka'ba-ye_Zartosht.JPG

Chapter 16. Canaanite Religion

Page 44 Ba'al and the Bull from blog of Rabbi Deborah Gordon http://blog.timesunion.com/rebdeb/yom-kippur-5772-the-bull-of-baal/834/

Chapter 17, Flood Stories from all over the world

Page 43 Noah's Ark http://en.wikipedia.org/wiki/Noah's_Ark

Page 67 Homeless man with Starbucks cup http://blogs.villagevoice.com/runninscared/homeless.jpeg

Page 68 Hosea by the German painter Eugen Spiro's series of Old Testament Prophets http://de.wikipedia.org/wiki/Eugene_Spiro#Werke_im_Besitz_von_Museen_und_.C3.B6ffentlichen_Institutionen

Chapter 26, Judaism: Meaningfulness

Page 70 Smith, Huston, *The World's Religions*, Harper-Collins, 1998

Page 70 David Friedman, *Ein Sof*, http://www.kosmic-kabbalah.com/ used with permission of the artist.

Page 72 Orthodox man and "hippie" at Western wall http://www.gorp.biz/?p=426

Chapter 27, Christianity: Jesus

Page 74 Smith, Huston, *The World's Religions*, Harper-Collins, 1998

Page 74 The Jesus Film http://www.jesusfilm.org

Page 75 Jesus crucified http://www.wikipaintings.org/en/antonello-da-messina/crusifixion-1475

Page 76 Jesus mosaic from a Roman Church ca 530 CE. Public Domain

Chapter 28, Christianity: Paul

Page 78 Wilson, A.N.: *Paul: The Mind Of The Disciple*, WW Norton, 1995.

Page 78 *Saul struck blind* by the University of Michigan bronze sculptor C. Malcolm Powers http://www-personal.umich.edu/~m-mpowrs/front.html

Page 79 Paul by Montagna http://upload.wikimedia.org/wikipedia/commons/e/ee/Bartolomeo_Montagna-Saint_Paul-Google_Art_Project.jpg

Page 80 Paul writing a letter by Valentin de Boulogne http://commons.wikimedia.org/wiki/File:File%22-Saint_Paul_Writing_His_Epistles%22_by_Valentin_de_Boulogne.jpg

Chapter 29, Christianity: Creeds And Heresies

Page 82 *The Transfiguration* by Raphael, modified.

Chapter 30, Christianity: Heaven And Hell

Chapter 31, Christianity: Branches On The Family Tree

Chapter 32 Islam: Muhammad and The Qur'an

Chapter 33: Islam: The Religion

Chapter 34, Sikhism: History and Theology

Chapter 35, Sikhism: Daily Life

Page 103 American tourists help make bread in Gurdwara http://www.flickr.com/photos/jbash/3829104066

Page 104 Sikh girl by Captain Suresh Sharma http://www.flickr.com/photos/79349001@N00/126241275

Page 105 *Bend it Like Beckham* http://www.imdb.com/title/tt0286499

Chapter 36, Mormonism

Page 106 Joseph Smith http://www.americankingswiki.com

Page 107 Temple in Salt Lake City http://upload.wikimedia.org/wikipedia/commons/9/93/Salt_Lake_Temple%2C_Utah_-_Sept_2004-2.jpg

Page 109 http://www.japantimes.co.jp/community/2012/10/23/issues/against-all-odds-mormons-in-japan-soldier-on/#.U0AMd61dUWY

Chapter 37, the Baha'i Faith

Page 111 Lotus temple http://countrylicious.com/india/images/6549986ffff96

Chapter 38, Christian Science

Page 112 Mary Baker Eddy http://www.daystarfoundation.org/wp-content/uploads/2013/01/MBE_about.png

Page 113 Mother Church http://www.breakingthethrees.com/2011/08/night-life-in-bostons-back-bay.html

Chapter 39, Ahmadiyya

Page 114 Ahmadiyya mosque in Calgary, Alberta http://www.ahmadiyyamosques.info/2011/12/baitun-nur-calgary-alberta-canada.html

Page 115 Ahmadiyya school in Sierra Leone, West Africa http://www.unicef.org/education/bege_61633.html

Chapter 40, Rastafari

Page 116 Lion of Judah monument in Addis Ababa, Ethiopia http://commons.wikimedia.org/wiki/File:Lion_of_Judah.JPG

Page 117 Haile Selassie http://en.wikipedia.org/wiki/File:Addis_Ababa-8e00855u.jpg

Page 118 Bob Marley http://wallpaperip.com/bob-marley-3418-hd-wallpapers.html

Epilogue

Page 119 Madre de Dios river and tributary system, near the Andes in Peru, NASA public domain. http://eoimages.gsfc.nasa.gov/images/imagerecords/7000/7394/madrededios_hydrosheds_lrg.jpg

CPSIA information can be obtained at www.ICGtesting.com
Printed in the USA
LVIW011938180920
666170LV00002B/9